SPIRITUAL
GUIDE
for
MAN

BOOK 1

MANNY RUDOLF

BALBOA.PRESS

A DIVISION OF HAY HOUSE

Balboa Press books may be ordered through booksellers or by contacting:

Balboa Press
A Division of Hay House
1663 Liberty Drive
Bloomington, IN 47403
www.balboapress.com
844-682-1282

Print information available on the last page.

ISBN: 979-8-7652-3288-0 (sc)
ISBN: 979-8-7652-3289-7 (hc)
ISBN: 979-8-7652-3287-3 (e)

Library of Congress Control Number: 2022914976

Balboa Press rev. date: 09/19/2022

CONTENTS

DEDICATION

This book is dedicated to all the beautiful souls who are on a spiritual path seeking to reconnect with their inner self, higher self, their spirit and soul.

May you awaken spiritually in this lifetime.

May we all attain a higher level of consciousness.

INTRODUCTION

Sleeping Man

The vast majority of people sleep through their waking lives unaware of the powers within them. Capable of attaining spiritual heights, they seem to prefer the great dream of life instead of awakening to the true reality of themselves as a spark of the divine. We are lost in a dream, some would call us the sleeping man. One has to exercise the force of will in order to wake oneself up in this lifetime. Other wise one drifts through life more or less in a sleep state missing most of the good stuff. When we say a sleep state, we mean not being in control, by allowing the body, the emotions, and the mind to be in control of our lives. Have you ever driven some place and when you arrived there, you realize you didn't remember the actual drive, or did you do something and then not realize that you did it. These are examples of operating in a sleep state. A great many of us are running on automatic. We do things and don't even know why we do these things. For most of us life is just one big habit or routine, we wake up in the morning, wash ourselves, eat breakfast, drive to work, do our daily work functions, drive home after work, make dinner, eat dinner, watch the television for several hours, and then finally we go to sleep. And we repeat this process at least five days a week. Of course weekends may be slightly different, but once again we most likely repeat the same activities, like shopping or watching sports on the television. So, at the end of our lives we realize we have done the same thing over and over without realizing why. It is sad to say that most of us are so busy in our daily routines that we are not even aware of our spirit. It is the goal of this book to put us back in touch with our spirit and back in control of our lives.

We are Spiritual Beings

We are spiritual beings. Most of us think we are human beings having a spiritual experience. However, it's actually the other way, we are spiritual beings having human experiences, not human beings having spiritual experiences. Many of us don't believe it and if we do, we don't really understand the obviousness of it. We don't believe it because we have been taught since birth that we are the human beings (the body, the emotions, and the mind), and that the spirit is some strange unknown. In fact most of us are never taught anything about the spirit. Even our educational system focuses on training the body and the mind, not the spirit. So it's no wonder that most of us know nothing about our spiritual side. Our nature as pure consciousness, as a spiritual being is right in front of us. Here is a brief exercise that will help you understand that you are a spiritual being. Close your eyes and picture a dog in your mind. What is looking at the dog? It's not the body, it's not the emotions, and it's not the mind. Here's another example. Close your eyes and notice your body. Notice that you can observe your body, the way your hands feel, your breathing, your feet on the ground. The simple obviousness is that there is a "you" observing your body. Next, do the same with your emotions. Notice the emotions in your body. Maybe you feel happy or sad, angry or calm, anxious or peaceful. The result is the same. There is a "you" observing your emotions. Next, do the same with your mind. Notice the thoughts in your mind. Maybe you're thinking of a show on television tonight or what to cook for dinner. The result is the same. There is a "you" observing your mind. You are that "you". The simple truth is, we are pure consciousness. We are not our body, our emotions, or our mind. This consciousness has a quality to it, it is love. We are pure love and we are nothing but goodness at the core. We are everything that we've ever wanted and most of us don't even know it. The problem is that our body, our emotions, and our minds are simply aligned with that which is not true. Our minds tell us that we're a body, that we're bad, unlovable, weak, pathetic, vulnerable, and evil, and our mind will fight to protect this. As pure consciousness, we are already free. It is our body, our emotions, and our mind that is not. The soul is who you are. The body, the emotions, and the mind are what you use to experience who you are in the physical realm.

Most of us allow the body, the emotions, and the mind to control our behavior and run our lives. Because we are not the body, the emotions, or the mind, we must learn to take back control of these parts of us and not let them control us. We must be in charge of and in control of the body, the emotions, and the mind. You would not start your car, put it into drive, and then let it go off on it's own, without guiding and steering it, would you? Well that's exactly what we allow our body, our emotions, and our mind to do. We have for too long given control to our body, our emotions, and our mind, thus allowing these parts of us to run and determine the outcome of our life. When we are not in control, the body, the emotions, and the mind hinder our connection to our spirit, thus giving us lives that we really do not want because the outcome of our lives is not in our control. This is what is happening to most of us. By taking control back we can determine the circumstances and outcome in our lives and regain that connection with our spirit.

In this book, we will learn how to be in control of our body, our mind, and our emotions. We will learn how to control our thoughts and be in charge of the thought process. We will learn how to control the creation process and create whatever we want in our lives. We will learn about meditation and how to connect with our higher self. We will learn about living in the present moment, also called the now. We will learn about mindfulness and how to practice this in our lives. We will learn about energy and vibrations, and how these impact our relationships and our lives. We will also learn to be in control of all aspects of our lives and how to create the life that you want using the law of attraction.

Some of the topics we will cover in this book are:

The Bodies
Breath
Meditation
Feelings and Emotions
The Mind
Thought

Mindfulness
Living in the Now
Energy
Vibrations
Law of Attraction
White light
Additional helpful information
Plus exercises for most of the above topics.

There are some main points that we will cover in this book as we are attempting to take back control of our body, our emotions, and our mind, and become spiritual beings having a human experience. These are the main points we will cover in this book and the things you will learn.

You will learn to take back control of your body.
You will learn to take back control of your emotions.
You will learn to take back control of your mind.
You will learn to turn off and quiet your mind.
You will learn to live in the now, not the past or the future.
You will learn about energy and vibrations, and how these impact us and our relationships.
We will learn about the law of attraction.
You will learn to connect with the force or flow of the universe and be one with everything.
You will learn to come from a place of love.
You will learn to only do things if they feel right for you, do not do things just because I tell you or someone else tells you to do them.
You will learn to train your mind and be in control of your thoughts.
You will learn to be in control of the creation process and create anything you want.
So, we should be able to create anything we want provided we follow the correct steps.

Most books give you a lot of theory, but no real practical applications. This book will provide both the theory and many exercises giving you the practical applications that will assist you in your life. It would be nice if we could do just one thing, one type of exercise like meditation to accomplish our goal. The truth is you need to work on multiple areas, you need to work on your whole being. It is through the use of breathing exercises, meditation, work with the emotions, exercises for the mind, work with thoughts, the use of mindfulness, the law of attraction, and work with energy and vibrations that we can regain the connection to our spirit, regain control of our lives, take back control of our lives, and determine our own destiny.

One of the greatest gifts you can give someone is your help. So I sincerely hope you will find this book a great help in reconnecting with your spiritual side. It is also my wish that this book help a great many people.

Reading Speed for this Book

It is suggested that you read one chapter per week and do all the exercises for that chapter each day of that week, this would allow you to finish the book in nine weeks. If you wish to go a little slower, you could read one chapter every two weeks. This will give you more time to work on the exercises. Do not rush these exercises and make sure you actually do all of the exercises. It takes twenty one days to make or break a habit, good or bad. So it is very important that you do these exercises and start building good habits. The chapters are intentionally short so that you can spend less time reading and have more time to do the exercises. The exercises in the first two or three chapters may seem very simple and easy to do, but please do them as we are building good habits and setting the foundation for all the future exercises in this book. You have to learn to walk before you can learn to run. We are attempting to take back control of our body, our emotions, and our mind. So it is best to start off simple, as the body, the emotions, and the mind will offer less resistance. If you attempt to make changes to quickly, the body, the emotions, and the mind will offer a great deal of resistance as they are afraid of change and are afraid of losing control of you. Thus a slower pace will be a great deal easier and you will experience less resistance. If the exercises seem to easy, please just do them anyway knowing they are building a solid foundation for you and that these exercises will help you with future exercises in this book. Once the book is completed you should continue to do the exercises mentioned in this book, as they will lead to greater spiritual understanding and spiritual growth, and help you create a better life. The breathing exercises, the meditations, the work with emotions, exercises for the mind, work with thoughts, the use of mindfulness, the law of attraction, and work with energy and vibrations are all activities you should do for the rest of your life. These are not activities that you do for two or three months and then stop, these are activities you do for a lifetime.

Look Up Definitions of Words Not Understood

An important note about words that are not understood. Have you ever read a page in a book and when you got to the bottom of the page you realize you didn't remember anything you just read. This is what happens when you go past a word you did not know the meaning or definition of. While you are reading this book or any book, if you come across any words that you do not understand, please look them up in a dictionary. This is important because confusion and the inability to grasp or learn comes right after a word that one did not understand has been skipped during reading. When a word is not grasped, the person then goes into a non comprehension or blankness of things immediately after. By not looking up the definition of these words you will have areas of this book that you do not remember or understand. This will hinder your understanding, comprehension, and learning of this material. So please look up any words so that you get the full understanding of this material. If you find that there comes a point where you do not remember what you have just read, or recently read, go back in the material to a point where you remember what you read and understood the material that you read. Then slowly read forward until you find the word you did not understand. Next look up the definition of the word and make sure you understand how it is being used in the sentence. Now read that sentence a second time. Then read forward from that point and you should understand the material. If you still do not understand the material, it means there is another word you do not understand. Just repeat the process of going back to a point where you understood the material that you were reading. Then begin reading slowly forward until you find the word you do not understand. Of course you would look up the definition of that word and read forward from that point, using the process just mentioned. This is a very important concept that one should use whenever reading material that you wish to understand and get the full comprehension of. So, please look up the definitions of the words you do not understand.

CHAPTER

The Two Sides of Man

There are two sides of man. We know that man is composed of two parts, the spirit which animates the body and the body itself. It is man's spiritual side that we are interested in here. Some would say that life is a journey. To create a better world, we must start with ourselves. Though no one can go back and make a brand new start, anyone can start from right now and make a brand new ending.

We are on this planet because we have lessons to learn, have promises or agreements to keep, or a service to perform, or need to further awaken to our relationship with the infinite. We are where we are in time and space, and our circumstances are what they are because of our habitual states of consciousness, mental states, choices, and personal behaviors. Considering the matter of fate, the law of cause and effect or karma, we should acknowledge that what we have experienced, thought, and done in the past has produced our present circumstances.

Many souls today have contact with the pure self. However, they have forgotten where they came from, and who they really are. Caught in the web of sense qualifications and gratifications, we return to this planet again and again, through action and reaction, to fulfill desires and work out past actions, until the day when we listen to that call from deep within, and begin our search for our true origin. To the degree that you realize the existence of spirit within your being, so will you rise in the spiritual scale of life. This is what spiritual development means.

As travelers in the cosmic ocean of life, we are fated to wander in time and space, and to experience a variety of impermanent relationships and circumstances until, having discovered the truth about ourselves, we awaken from the dream of mortality and fulfill our spiritual destiny. Experiences of repeated physical birth and death continue until we out grow our attachments to this realm by awakening to higher realities. Souls are destined to awaken from the dream of mortality to full realization of god. It is just a question of how long it will take us to reach full realization of god. We earn a place in the next world by the way we have lived in this world.

The Bodies

Man is a soul and has a body, several bodies in fact, for besides the visible vehicle (physical body) by means of which he transacts his business with his lower world, he has other bodies which are not visible to ordinary sight, by means of which he deals with the higher worlds.

In yoga, the layers of our selves are called "Maya koshas". Literally, maya means illusion and a kosha is a body sheath, a layer, a covering. So the masters conceptualized the self as not one body but five distinct bodies layered on top of one another that cover the pure light of the highest self. Each body is a distinct maya kosha, or kosha for short. Each kosha is made up of increasingly finer energy vibrations as you move inward. We can see the physical body which is the outer most layer, but the other four bodies are energy states invisible to the naked eye. If you pay attention, you can sense and feel their presence within you. The five bodies form a covering for the pure self, or light within. These sheaths are often compared to layers of an onion, over time they become

2

so thick and hardened that they completely cover what's within. They become the obstacles that hinder us from experiencing the light within. Some of us have trouble conceptualizing this inner light. Some people think of this deepest part of us as the soul, others call it god within, or their highest self. The first body is your physical body which we are all familiar with, this is the outer most body, the one you see. Your second body is your energy or breathing body. Becoming aware of your flow of breathing is the first step in contacting your energy or breathing body and a way into awareness of the deeper koshas. The third body is the mental or emotional body, of the mind, senses, and emotions. Thoughts, feelings, and all that you perceive from the five senses reside within this kosha. Breathing techniques help keep this body in balance. Your fourth body, subtler still, is called your wisdom body. Your fifth body is called your bliss body. This is the subtlest body, the thinnest layer, which stands between ordinary awareness and the state of stillness, peace, bliss, and the light existing within us all. It helps to visualize them as layers, one on top of the other, with the first layer, the physical body, on the outside, and the others layered successively within.

The first body is your physical body which we are all familiar with. This is also known as the food body. The food that you eat today becomes the hair, skin, and teeth of tomorrow. Our physical body is stressed and affected by many things. You need to pay attention to how you feel. Exercise helps the body deal with stress and relaxes the body. Sufficient water and good food are needed to keep the body running and healthy. Relaxation is also very helpful for the body

Your second body is your energy or breathing body. Becoming aware of your flow of breathing is the first step in contacting your energy or breathing body and a way into awareness of the deeper koshas. This is your energy body, sometimes called your breath body. Prana is the energy associated with our breathing, often called "Breath of life". While the energy body is closely associated with the physical function of breathing, it is not considered to be a physical part of ourselves. It's a sort of human energy field made up of our mental, emotional, psychological, and spiritual currents. This energy or current called prana, is likened to fuel that feeds and circulates through the physical body and mind, in the same way that our breath does. Pranayama is the breathing practice, this enhances the circulation of prana to all levels of the koshas. We can influence the flow of our prana energy by focusing on specific positive things and by intentionally changing our breathing patterns. Yoga students use a series of breathing techniques called pranayama to exercise, refuel, and replenish vitality to the koshas. Prana is a concept that means energy or life force and is usually associated with our breathing. Pranayama is often referred to as controlling ones breath. In pranayama we purposefully extend or shorten our breathing patterns with the intention of affecting the flow of our prana. Illness could be looked at as the improper flow of prana, and the absence of prana is death. Prana exists in all living things.

The third body is the mental or emotional body, of the mind, senses, and emotions. Thoughts, feelings, and all that you perceive from the five senses reside within this kosha. Breathing techniques help keep this body in balance. This is the mental body, sometimes called the emotional body. A person is full of thoughts, feelings, and emotions. In this body we store everything we have learned, felt, and perceived. All sense perceptions are stored in this body sometimes called the "Body made of thought". This kosha carries the scars of past wounds, stressful thoughts, memories, hurts, and pains. As we age this kosha becomes increasingly burdened with all the stress and injuries of the past and present. Breathing and relaxation are enormously helpful in keeping your mental body healthy. The mental body feeds on the energy of obsessive thinking, stressful thinking, and the sense impressions we feed it. If we keep supplying this kosha with a continual stream of violent and bad news, stressful and confused thinking, and troublesome relationships, the mental body begins to crave increased forms of this insidious energy. Your mental or emotional body is a living history of all the things you like and dislike, as well as your fears, hopes, desires, and so on. One of the best things we can do for our mental or emotional body is to be careful what we feed it. The mental or emotional body is sometimes called the pain body. This pain body affects our everyday lives, robbing us of peace and the freedom to enjoy life. Meditation helps to quiet the mind and balance the emotions, thus calming the mental or emotional body.

Your fourth body is called your wisdom body. Your wisdom body is your body of higher wisdom, judgment, and discernment. Developing this kosha means tapping into your deep inner reservoir of knowledge and intuition. This is where your will power lies. This is where you get strength of character. A very powerful and effective way to connect with your wisdom body is through meditation. Meditation is simply the practice of bringing your body and mind into a deep state of calm. As meditation and relaxation practice deepens, your ability to connect with your wise inner guidance is enhanced.

Your fifth body is called your bliss body. This is the thinnest layer, which stands between ordinary awareness and the state of stillness, peace, bliss, and the light existing within us all. It helps to visualize them as sheaths, one on top of the other, with the first sheath or layer, the physical body, on the outside, and the other layered successively within. The deepest, innermost layer, the fifth sheath, is your bliss body. This sheath is extremely important because it is the final and thinnest layer that stands between ordinary awareness and our higher self. Feelings (not to be confused with emotions) such as stillness, love, peace, and contentment are often experienced at this sheath. The bliss body is the finest and thinnest layer that stands between ordinary awareness and our higher self.

When you sleep your physical body rests and repairs itself. In dreams your emotional body carries out its wishes, hopes, fears, and fantasies. Your being returns to the world of light, which some people perceive as heaven. The reason we go to sleep at night is so that we can put all these bodies in order after the exertions of being awake and active. But the subtlest work of all is done in pure silence. The next time you notice a passing moment of quietness when you have no thoughts or feelings or desires, do not take it as absentmindedness, your awareness has slipped between the cracks of the physical, energy, mental, wisdom, and bliss bodies. In deep silence we return to the ultimate cause or pure being.

It is through the use of breathing exercises, meditation, work with the emotions, exercises for the mind, work with thoughts, the use of mindfulness, and work with energy and vibrations that we can regain the connection to our spirit, regain control of our lives, and take back control of our lives, thus determining our own destiny.

Breath

There is no single more powerful or more simple daily practice to further your health and well being than breath work. Breath is the great purifier, filling the blood with oxygen which each cell requires for internal breathing and repair. You know that good blood circulation is necessary for the well being of your body. The same is true for the psyche, you must live and practice in such a way that your consciousness benefits from good circulation. The psyche is the totality of elements forming the mind. Bad circulation of psychological elements creates problems, causing blocks of suffering, fear, pain, and distress which are stuck in the depths of your consciousness, they can not circulate, and they make you feel emotions like fear. That's why you have closed the door to your consciousness, because you do not want these things to come to the surface. You are afraid of the pain within you, and so whenever there is a gap in your day, you fill it up with things like sports or television so these blocks of suffering do not come up to the surface. In this way you create bad psychological circulation, and mental problems will soon appear. The cells of your body are not only physical, they are also mental, they are both at the same time.

It may seem like a very simple thing to do, but has anyone ever taught you how to breath correctly, most likely the answer is no. Correct breath is very important to our physical well being, our emotional state, our mental state, and our spiritual state. Breath work helps calm the body, the emotions, the mind, and the spirit.

Breathing Exercise:

This breathing exercise is called "Count". Do this breathing exercise for five to ten minutes several times daily. Count silently, not out loud. Inhale slowly through your nose, count 1-2-3-4-5-6 as you are inhaling, hold the breath while counting 1-2-3-4-5-6, exhale slowly through the mouth while counting 1-2-3-4-5-6, repeat this process for five to ten minutes several times a day for the entire week. Again, count silently, not out loud. All we are doing here is putting our attention on our breath and of course counting our breaths. We should focus our attention on our breathing.

The exercises in the first two or three chapters may seem very simple and easy to do, but please do them as we are building good habits and setting the foundation for all the future exercises in this book. We are attempting to take back control of the body, the emotions, and the mind, so it is best to start off simple, as the body, the emotions, and the mind will offer less resistance. If you attempt to make changes to quickly, the body, the emotions, and the mind will offer a great deal of resistance as they are afraid of change and are afraid of losing control of you. Thus a slower pace will be a great deal easier and you will experience less resistance. So if these exercises seem to easy, please just do them anyway knowing they are building a solid foundation for you and that these exercises will help you with future exercises in this book.

Meditation

Meditation means to think or look inwardly toward the soul, rather that outwardly through the senses. Meditation should not be practiced with the intention of our trying to get something. We should practice in order to be. Meditation is a form of private devotion in which the mind concentrates on a particular practice which frees it from its normal thoughts. Meditation is the main vehicle for deepening one's spiritual life. Meditation is your way of staying connected to the higher self, to spirit, to god.

We may have many experiences and play a great variety of roles but the secret of true happiness lies in our ability to always know who we are, not the personality, the body, the emotions, the mind, or karmic patterns. Meditation and self acceptance guarantees liberation.

Meditation Exercise:

Meditation is stopping, calming the mind, and concentrating. Looking deeply within to get insight. First you focus your mind on something like your steps, concentrate on your steps, mindful of something. So for this exercise walk around slowly and put all your attention on your steps. Try to keep your mind and thoughts on your steps. Do this meditation for five to ten minutes everyday. At first this will be very difficult as your mind will try to pull you in all different directions, but keep practicing this meditation as it will get easier as you spent more time attempting to concentrate on your steps. When your mind pulls you somewhere else, just gently bring your attention back to your steps.

Next try focusing your attention on your breath, be mindful of your breath. So mindful or mindfulness means being aware and focusing on something. Sit in a comfortable position or lay down, breathe in, breathe out, keeping your attention on your breath. Try to keep your mind and thoughts on your breathing. Continue this meditation for five to ten minutes and you will experience insight. Again, when your mind pulls you somewhere else, just gently bring your attention back to your breath. Do this meditation for five to ten minutes everyday.

Everyday, do both of these meditations, alternating the focus on your steps with the focus of your breath.

Attention

What you put your attention on grows stronger in your life. Put your attention on all the good in your life. Your life is created first in your mind and then in the world. So attention is what you focus your mind on.

Intention

Quantum physics suggests that the universe is primarily empty space, and that the things we perceive as real are simply a matter of one's individual perception, it is also hypothesized that matter can be affected by intention (prayer, wishes, concentration, visualization, and so forth).

Intention is what you wish to accomplish or achieve. You can control your own destiny. You must have clear intentions. Intention creates attention. Set an intention, what you want to be, do, or have,

The clearer your intention the better your results. Once you are clear on your intention, the only thing you need to pay attention to and invest your time in are those things that support your intention. Whatever you give energy to is what you will have more of. Our intention is our overall purpose. Intention creates attention and the expansion of possibilities that will come to us. Intention is why we choose our direction. Why we do something is more important than how we do it, the why is our intention. The key to success is to have dominant thought patterns that are totally aligned with what you want. This is our creative intention.

Mind

The phenomenon we call mind is the primary source of tension in our body, our emotions, and our daily lives. The mind forms a veil, an obscured lens, through which we see reality. We tend to accept these distorted perceptions as true and real until we realize that the mind itself is the mischief maker, the trickster, and the trouble maker who weaves illusions while hiding in our psyche, whispering as friend and trusted adviser. The psyche is the totality of elements forming the mind. The mind is like a reflex organ that reacts to everything and fills your head with thousands of random thoughts everyday, none of which are of any importance.

You have a brain that directs the body, stores information, and plays with that information. We refer to the brain's abstract processes as the intellect. The brain and the mind are not the same. The brain is real, the mind isn't. "Mind" is the illusory reflection of cerebral fidgeting. It comprises all the random, uncontrolled thoughts that bubble into awareness from the subconscious. Consciousness is not mind, awareness is not mind, attention is not mind. Mind is an obstruction, an aggravation. It is a kind of evolutionary mistake in the human being, a primary weakness in the human experience.

The mind is the creator of illusion. The mind, or the mental body is the result of past thinking, and is constantly being modified by present thinking. It is a thing, precise and definite with certain powers and capacities, strength and weakness, which are the outcome of activities in this life and previous lives. It is as we have made it. The results of our past thinking are present with us as mind, and each mind has its own rate of vibration, and is in a state of perpetual motion, offering an ever changing series of thoughts and pictures.

In the building and evolution of our minds we must steadily work at right thinking, for we are our own builders. Thus the need for controlling our mind. Thought alone builds the mind. If your mind is filled with negative attitudes and thoughts, it will be difficult to entertain positive attitudes and thoughts. But if your mind is filled with positive attitudes and thoughts, it will be difficult for negative ones to enter.

One way of helping the growth of the mind body is the practice of concentration, that is, the fixing of the mind on a point and holding it there firmly not allowing it to drift or wander. We should train ourselves in thinking steadily and consecutively, not allowing our minds to run suddenly from one thing to another, not to waste our energies away over a large number of insignificant thoughts.

The device used for focusing the mind is the faculty of concentration, or attention directed by will. Developing powers of concentration is equivalent to developing muscular strength. Anyone can do it, it merely takes exercise and practice. Your goal is control of the mind, the three main points are meditation, concentration, and visualization, so that you can focus your attention on one point, and be free from distractions. The mental or mind body of the next incarnation depends on the work we are doing in the mental or mind body of the present. The more we do now, the better will be our future lifetimes.

Mind Exercise:

Suspend a needle by a silk thread, and then learn to move it by the force of the will. To do this, hang a silk thread from the ceiling of the room, or from a high object so the thread can swing freely. A needle should be at the end of the thread. Concentrate on that needle and try to move it with the power of your mind. When developed, mental waves can move this needle. Work five to ten minutes daily on this exercise for the entire week. In the beginning, the needle at the end of the thread will not move. With time, you will see that the needle oscillates and moves. This exercise is to develop mental power. Remember mental waves travel through space and pass from one mind to the next.

Additional Helpful Information – Walk and Look

This exercise is called "Walk and Look". When you are feeling tired or exhausted, or feeling closed in and internalized, or feeling upset for some reason, or just feeling unhappy, or your outlook on life is declining, you should go outside and take a walk for ten or fifteen minutes until you feel better. When I say take a walk, I mean go outside and walk around the block, not walk around the inside of your house. While taking a walk look around at the people and things that you see, look at things close and things far away. This will move you from an internalized state to an externalized state. This will correct these imbalances and improve your outlook on life. You will wake up, feel refreshed, and feel better because of this. If you are sitting in front of a computer screen all day, or doing other similar work, you will become introverted. One should spend some time being extroverted after having introverted all day. So any time you are not feeling refreshed or your outlook on life is declining, go out and take a nice walk around the block for ten or fifteen minutes and look around to improve your outlook on life. The body moving increases the blood flow which causes us to wake up, and the looking around at things puts our attention on things outside of ourselves. This will make you feel much more refreshed and improve your outlook on life. I would ask you to take a walk right now for ten or fifteen minutes and follow the instructions above for "Walk and Look" and see how you feel after wards. You should use this in the future whenever you are feeling tired or exhausted, or feeling closed in and internalized, or feeling upset for some reason, or just feeling unhappy, or your outlook on life is declining. I would suggest that every time you go for a walk outdoors, you use "Walk and Look" to put you in an externalized state, this will improve your outlook and beingness. "Walk and Look" really works, try it.

CHAPTER

The Universe

In the world of physical matter, everything is made up of molecules, atoms, and electrons. Every particle of physical matter is in a continuous state of highly agitated motion. Nothing is ever still, although to the eye, all physical matter may appear to be motionless. There is no solid physical matter. The hardest piece of metal is really an organized mass of revolving molecules, atoms, and electrons. All matter is in a constant state of vibration or motion. The molecule is made up of rapidly moving particles called atoms, and the atom is made up of rapidly moving particles called electrons. This is the vibrating nature or fluid of matter. In every particle of matter there is an invisible force which causes the atoms to circle around one another at an inconceivable rate of speed. We can call this vibration. It is believed that the rate of speed with which matter vibrates determines to a large extent the nature of the outward visible appearance of the physical objects in the universe.

As far as the world is concerned, everything is structured in consciousness and there is an order to things. We know that man is composed of two parts, the spirit which animates the body and the body itself. Human beings operate within a magnetic field. All that we perceive now or might perceive in the future has to do with the manifest worlds which are illusory in nature.

It is not necessary to search for anything outside of oneself. The journey is not outside, but inside, being or becoming aware of inner space, or the inner dimension of consciousness. Humans have become lost in the outer physical dimension, and have forgotten the inner dimension. There are two primary dimensions that we will be concerned with, the outer physical dimension and the inner spiritual dimension. These two dimensions are manifested and unmanifested. We need to become aware of both of these dimensions. Most of us are only aware of the manifested or outer physical dimension. Welcome to the human condition.

Earth is ascending, our consciousness is also ascending. We are remembering that we are beings of light and love, who are one with everything and god. Try to feel this connection to the universe.

Holographic Reality

When you look in the mirror, what do you see? Do you see the real you or what you have been conditioned to believe is you? The two are so very different. One is an infinite consciousness capable of being and creating whatever it chooses, the other is an illusion imprisoned by its own perceived and programmed limitations. Which of the "you's" is controlling your life? The world you see through your eyes is a holographic three dimensional virtual reality created by oneness as a vast experience.

There is a three dimensional, virtual reality, holographic, movie screen designed to provide us with an opportunity to experience the separation of oneness as an aid to further our exploration of ourselves. We arc all aspects of one consciousness, god, experiencing itself subjectively through its constituent parts. Again, it is not necessary to search for anything outside of oneself. The journey is not outside but inside.

Reality

Maya is the world of illusion. Maya means illusion. Success on the spiritual path is a matter of carefully directed attention. Few realize the subtle processes which must be undergone. Our over identification with externals and the consciousness clouding effect of maya prevents us from knowing who and what we are. People who identify with maya (the fabric of nature, space, time, and energy) to the extent that they are no longer aware of their soul nature, are delusional. It is only an illusion that a material world exists outside and separate from you.

The three levels or planes of existence are the physical, mental, and spiritual. Each plane vibrates at different rates, and these vibrational differences are the only distinguishing factors between planes. The higher spiritual planes vibrate the fastest, and the lower material planes vibrate the slowest, which is why matter appears dense and solid. Each plane is divided into subcategories and is subdivided from lower to higher vibrations. The universe is in constant motion at different vibrations. The only variable separating one plane from another is its vibration. The higher the vibrational rate, the higher the plane.

The individual mind narrows our awareness down, as if we are looking at the world through a peep hole. This is the illusion of reality. All that we see or have seem is but a dream within a dream. You realize that the world is in you, and not you in the world. As far as the world is concerned, everything is constructed in consciousness. The impression that your consciousness exists at a particular place in the world is an illusion. Everything we experience in this world is an illusion. Everything we experience is a construct within consciousness. Our sense of being a unique self is merely another construct of the mind. We place this image of the self at the center of our perceived world, giving us the sense of being in the world. But the truth is just the opposite. It is all within us. Life is made of two realms, there is the inner world, and there is the outer world. Most of us only operate in the outer world, and don't even realize there is an inner world. We need to be connected to the inner world if we are to find our way back to who we really are.

Evidence from nearly every direction points to the existence of dimensions other that the one in which we now primarily focus our consciousness. As reality is multidimensional, so is consciousness.

Heaven

Heaven is not a place, but a state of consciousness. Heaven is in another dimension. When we die we move into that other dimension. All principles of heaven and earth are living inside you. Ancient texts say that "The kingdom of heaven is within you" and what they're talking about is the frequency or vibrational level of your being. The light is all about you, you have only to cast the bondage from your eyes and look. But what is this casting away of a bondage? It is simply a question of raising consciousness to a higher level by learning to focus it in finer matter or higher vibration. "The kingdom of heaven is within you", simply means, raise your vibrational level to become aware of and find heaven.

Hell

The concept of hell is an evil doctrine that originated in pagan mythology. It was later used by the church to put fear in the minds of people so the church could control the people and get donations. It is documented that church officials would charge people fees for the forgiveness of their sins. Hell does not exist and never did. It was created and used to control people and get money from the people a very long time ago and unfortunately it is still being used today by some churches. I have heard it said that living your life at a very low vibrational level is like living in hell. We will talk much more about vibrational levels in this book.

Matter

Matter is derived from mind and not mind from matter. All matter is merely energy condensed to a slow vibration. Thought is real, physical is the illusion. Matter is a dense form of energy with a slower rate of vibration. The material plane is composed of vibrating molecules. If a material object was vibrating fast enough, the human senses would no longer see or hear the object. The object would leave the material plane and move upward in frequency to the mental and spiritual planes. This is how masters appear and disappear, they raise or lower their vibrational level.

The Veil of Matter

Most human beings possess a mental screen that keeps us from seeing beyond "The veil of matter". All that we perceive now or might perceive in the future has to do with the manifest worlds which are illusory in nature. It is only an illusion that a material world exists outside and separate from you. Remember the material universe is not real. Since this world is an illusion anyway, we should be able to create anything we want provided we follow the correct steps.

Waking Up

It is not necessary to search for anything outside of oneself. The journey is not outside but inside, this is the way out. Bodhi is awakening, enlightenment, which means "To wake up". To become aware of what is going on within and all around you. We are on this planet because we have lessons to learn, have promises or agreements to keep, or services to perform, or need to further awaken to our relationship with the infinite. Realization of one's divine nature brings release from the trap of one's animal nature, often called the "Mind body trap", which causes subjectivity and limited vision. All transformation is a result of a conscious change in our thinking. This means that we must train ourselves to select and control our thoughts. The soul seeks freedom from the prison of negative thinking. The soul is composed of our thoughts. Any change in our thinking immediately affects the soul. We can not master our lives unless we master our minds. And we can not master our minds if we do not personally examine them. Without mastery of the mental processes there can be no realization and no awakening.

If one person gains spiritually, the whole world gains. Most people operate in a state of autopilot. We must wake up from this state of autopilot. We must wake up and make each of our choices consciously. When we slip into unconsciousness and forget our deepest desires, we fall into an automatic trance collapsing into past programming and patterns, this is life going on autopilot. The trance takes us from one moment to the next, taking us on the road to nowhere. Were asleep at the wheel, letting our past and our fears dictate and limit out futures. People hypnotize themselves by listening to the thoughts in their head, so they're in a kind of trance, and they're not really aware of anything around them. People are lost in this trance state, listening to the thoughts in their head. If you are walking around asleep, in a trance state and you're not alert, you miss the guidance, information, and messages that are constantly speaking to you, guiding and directing you in your life. The world is full of sleep walkers on autopilot. If we are eating and thinking about business, we are dreaming, because we are doing one thing and thinking about another. When we stop dreaming in the physical world, we awaken. It is painful to know that the consciousness of all human beings sleeps and dreams profoundly in both the hours of rest of the physical body, and also during the hours of non rest, our waking hours. Most physical beings are so completely integrated into their physical world that they have very little conscious awareness of their relationship with the non physical world.

We have two paths. The path of consciousness where we choose our future or the path of unconsciousness where the future is created from the past, which does not move us any closer to our dreams. We should practice being present and awaken from the dream of thought, this will allow us to step out of that dream and awaken into awareness. Spiritual awakening is the awakening from the dream of thought.

As travelers in the cosmic ocean of life, we are fated to wander in time and space and to experience a variety of impermanent relationships and circumstances until, having discovered the truth about ourselves, we awaken from the dream of mortality and fulfill our spiritual destiny.

Satori

A zen concept, satori occurs when attention rests in the present moment, when the body is alert, sensitive, relaxed, and the emotions are open and free. Satori is the warriors state of being. Sports, exercise, dance, music, and any other challenging activity can serve as a gateway to satori. This requires full attention to your actions. Satori should become your everyday reality.

Chuang Tzu's dream, Chuang Tzu fell asleep and dreamed he was a butterfly. Upon awakening he asked himself, "Am I a man who dreamed that he was a butterfly, or a sleeping butterfly now dreaming that he is a man".

Focus your mind and free your emotions, then expand this clarity into daily life until satori becomes your everyday reality. Focus and keep your attention on the present moment, on what you are doing in the present moment. Satori is your key to the gate. Every moment – satori. Enlightenment is not an attainment, it is a realization.

Meditate your actions. Meditating an action is different from doing it. To do, there is a doer, a self conscious someone performing. But when you meditate an action, you've already released attachment to outcomes. There's no you left to do it. In forgetting yourself, you become what you do, so your action is free, spontaneous, without ambition, inhibition, or fear.

Many Years Ago

Many years ago, far in the past, there were these intelligent spiritual beings that were all powerful and lived in the now, lived in the moment, lived in peace and harmony. These beings thought it would be fun to create and experience a physical reality. They created a playground called the material plane or physical reality or material world. While this physical reality is an illusion, they found great pleasure playing in this physical reality. However, they kept playing in this physical reality so much, that they forgot who they really were and where they really came from. Somewhere along the way, they had an idea to create something that could do things for them without putting much attention on things. Kind of like a program in a computer, you tell it what to do and it does it. Then they gave it the ability to reason and make decisions, and remember things (memory). They called this device the mind. At first it was fun to have this new device do things automatically. As time went on and they gave the mind more things to do, it started to run on its own, without the being requesting it to do so. Soon the being found the mind was constantly rerunning old programs or old events. Particularity events that caused them pain and made them feel bad. Then the mind started to project these feelings into their future thoughts and soon they felt emotions like fear, worry, and regret based on things the mind was showing them or replaying for them. Where once there was peace and silence, now there was great noise, mental noise. Soon peace and silence were gone completely and the mind was running out of control causing these being all kinds of imaginary problems. The mind had gained control, or should we say the beings had lost control of the mind. Some refer to this as the ego, the mind out of control. Some beings had such a difficult time with this that they turned to things like sex, alcohol, and drugs in an attempt to quiet their mind. This mind is what plagues us today and has for a great many years, maybe even millions or billions of years. So what is one to do? We must learn to quiet the mind and take back control of the mind.

Once again, the soul is who you are, the body and the mind are what you use to experience who you are in the physical realm. It is through the use of breathing exercises, meditation, work with the emotions, exercises for the mind, work with thoughts, the use of mindfulness, and work with energy and vibrations that we can regain the connection to our spirit, regain control of our lives, take back control of our lives, and determine our own destiny.

Prana

Prana is vital life force. The word prana means vital life force or energy. Prana is energy that comes through the breath, often called "Breath of life". This is not just the energy of the human being, but the cosmic electrical currents which man and all creatures assimilate and transmit as part of the great flow of divine life. Prana is the energy that creates life, mind, and matter. Our bodies draw prana in through our nostrils as we breathe. Prana flows through the physical body in subtle channels known as nadis. Prana is distributed throughout the body by these nadis, channels of energy. We have three prana storage centers, like batteries in the body. The first is about two inches below the naval, the second is at the heart, and the third is in the center of the forehead. When you guide your prana into positive channels you can begin to master your mind.

Pranayama

Pranayama is conscious breath control. Pranayama means directing and control of the vital forces of the body through conscious regulation of the breathing mechanism. We use breathing techniques to gain control over our physical body, our mind and our subtle energy. Subtle energy is prana.

Breath

Its the breath that quiets the mind for meditation. Breath is the key. If we control the breath, we control the mind and the body. The breath is the master of the mind and body. Breath is the connection between mind and body. You know how to do this, one deep in breath, one gentle out breath, and the body and mind come together. Breath is the bridge which connects life to consciousness, which unites your body to your thoughts. Whenever your mind becomes scattered use your breath as the means to take hold of your mind again. By slowing down the rate of breathing to fifteen breathes or less per minute, it is possible to change the speed of the mind. Breath work helps rise awareness, and helps turn your direction away from the physical world to the non physical world.

Most people breathe in a very shallow manner, denying the body its full supply of oxygen and weakening their defense against emotional stress. Practice abdominal breathing. Breathe deeply, allowing any tension you may be holding to drain from your body. Belly or abdominal breathing brings in prana energy, chest breathing depletes prana energy.

I know a person who takes very shallow breaths using only their upper chest while breathing. Due to this incorrect breathing practice, this person has become a very nervous person full of anxiety. Whenever this person does any type of exertion like work or exercise, they sound like a panting dog. One can calm the nerves just by using a correct breathing technique. We will start off easy and work our way up to correct breathing techniques.

Breathing Exercise:

This breathing exercise is called "Abdominal breathing". Do this breathing exercise for five to ten minutes several times daily. Sit in a comfortable position or lay down. In order to take the fullest breath, you have to do what is called abdominal breathing, that is when you take a deep breath, your belly should move outward. To find out whether this is happening, just put your hand on your abdomen and see if it moves outward as you take a breath. Many of us do not let our abdomens expand freely as we breathe. We restrict those muscles, and as a result are unable to take a full, deep breath. So practice just taking some deep breaths and letting your belly move outward. Only when that movement occurs are you taking the full volume of air into your lungs that you are capable of taking. The abdominal breathing exercise is one you can do informally, any time, while waiting in line, sitting at a stoplight, watching TV, or listening to a lecture. The goal would be to do abdominal breathing all the time making his our normal breathing routine or habit, so that you can always get a full breath and a full supply of energy from your breathing. Please do this breathing exercise several times everyday this week.

Meditation

The ultimate goal of meditation is a state of awareness in which you temporarily lose self identity and merge with all that is. Meditation is communing with god for the purpose of working knowingly with god. Your whole body and entire being changes when you practice meditation regularly. Use meditation techniques to calm physical and mental processes and to internalize attention, then let meditation unfold without conscious effort on your part. In many ways meditation charges the batteries both on the inner spiritual and outer physical levels. Meditation brings you back to yourself, to your deepest nature. The breath is the tool, awareness is the vehicle. Awareness and breath joining into spirit. Meditation can prepare you for a good nights sleep and for the dream state. There are many breathing techniques to relax you in preparation for either meditation or sleep.

Meditation Exercise:

This is a breathing meditation. Do this breathing meditation for five or ten minutes several times daily. Sit in a comfortable position or lay down. Using abdominal breathing, breathe in the life that is all around you, breath deeply with the natural rhythm of life for several minutes, sit or lay quietly. As you inhale feel yourself taking in the energy of life, then after awhile imagine this energy of life entering through a portal at the top of your head as you inhale. Then watch this energy go through your body and exit through your feet as you exhale. Do this for five or ten minutes or until you feel enlightened. Please do this meditation several times everyday this week.

Mind

When we say "Be still and know that I am god", the "Be still" means quiet the mind, stop the thoughts.

When you stop the thoughts, when you quiet the mind, you start to get back in touch with the real you, the true you, the powerful peaceful being that you once were. The "Know that I am god" means you begin to connect or should I say reconnect with your true self. As you start to reconnect everything in your life will start to change, start to get better, and improve. You will find you are happier, you will find things are attracted to you, things like love, happiness, money, and success.

Your mind is like a lake, its surface broken only by the ripples of thought that pass over it. In order to see the self who lays beneath, first you must learn to still the ripples, to become the master of your mind rather than the servant. People who do terrible things, who harm others, do so because of all the excessive uncontrolled thoughts or mental noise, it can drive a person crazy. This mental noise causes people to seek relief from things like sex, alcohol, and drugs. Take control back from the mind, stop the thoughts, shut down the mind, do not give it any more power.

There was a comedian who joked and said, "The mind is a terrible thing and must be stopped in this lifetime", little did he know how true this really is. The mind has really become a terrible thing and yes we do need to stop it, the sooner, the better.

You have to learn to select your thoughts everyday, this is a power that you can cultivate. Work on the mind, that's the only thing you should be trying to control. If you can't master your thoughts, your in trouble forever. You are in control of your mind and therefore your results. The entire universe is a product of your mind. Most people are unaware that they possess this power. When your thoughts are positive and elevated, you attract and manifest more desirable outcomes. As mentioned, by slowing down the rate of breathing to fifteen breathes or less per minute, it is possible to change the speed of the mind and slow it down.

Clearing the Mind

Encased in the bodily prison, the soul consciousness and life force identifies with the physical vehicle and its mortal limitations. Spirituality is the awakening of divinity in consciousness. It is the supreme good of consciousness in human beings which frees the consciousness from the "Mind body trap". This freedom is obtained by a gradual process of transformation of the sense consciousness of the mind. It takes time for the centuries old accumulation of debris to be cleaned out of the mind and consciousness. It is sense consciousness that perceives the world and that constantly produces uncontrolled thoughts. By transforming the sense consciousness one can achieve freedom from the slavery of the mind, internal dialogue, uncontrolled thoughts, and the uncontrolled mind trapped by desires that leads to bondage. A person on the spiritual path eventually attains salvation, that level of understanding and inward realization where he knows himself to be a soul which is but using mind and body for a purpose. Souls are destined to awaken from the dream of mortality to full realization of god.

Thoughts

Most people are not in control of their own thoughts, and constantly bombard their higher self with an uncontrolled and contradictory mixture of plans, wishes, and fears. This confuses the higher self and is why most people's lives appear to be equally haphazard and uncontrolled, thus they don't get what they want. Most people spend there entire life imprisoned within the confines of their own thoughts. They never go beyond a narrow self created, mind made sense of self that is conditioned by the past. Most people are not aware that we can control our state of mind by controlling our thoughts. All things that are manifested are preceded by the manifestation of thought, nothing just happens. Everything that happens is a vibrational response to a pattern of thought. Spiritually awakening is awakening from the dream of thought.

You were born to live a good life, and you should start focusing your thoughts on things that will allow you to live a good life. That which you give your thought to is that which you begin to invite into your experience. You get what you are thinking about, whether it is something you want or something you do not want. Negative thoughts create negative results and positive thoughts create positive results.

Every definite thought produces two effects, first a radiating vibration, second a floating form. Thoughts are tangible things, a finer form of matter. Your thoughts create your destiny. Thought is the builder. A thought is energy that never dies and lasts forever. Like energy attracts like energy. Learn to control your thoughts, for thought is energy. Mental images are concentrated energy. Thoughts produce a dual effect, a vibration and a form. This vibration is a wave of feeling that comes from the mind of the thinker. This vibration is also known as a thought wave. Vibrations tend to impact the minds of others who are vibrating at a similar frequency. Every vibration is instantly followed by a form, which is a picture. This is known as a thought form. Thought forms are mental pictures in the mind.

Your thoughts and images regarding yourself have a powerful impact on your health. Many people do not understand how thought and health are linked. All illness and all wellness are equally the result of the way we think. Thoughts and feelings affect our emotional body and create vibrations of harmony or disharmony. This in turn affects the physical body. When we keep our thoughts constructive, positive, kind, and loving, we are happy. Happiness brings harmony, and living in harmony creates health. Disease is the result of living in disharmony. Anger, fear, anxiety, frustration, disappointment, worry, and stress create thought forms that break down the physical body and make us sick. Many times, illnesses like the common cold and flu are brought upon us because our immune system is weakened as a result of emotional stress. The root cause of our emotional stress can be found in our thinking. When a thought is held for a prolonged period it will manifest. Any thought or emotion held and repeated will bring an equal result. Anger, fear, hatred, bitterness, resentment, and jealousy create powerful thought forms and always result in either a physical or mental disease or disorder. Telling lies also creates negative thought forms which hang around for awhile. Our thinking has an enormous affect on our health. A healthy diet, taking vitamins, exercising, and not smoking or abusing drugs or alcohol will help you remain healthy. But it takes right thinking to live a healthy life.

When negative thoughts come into your mind, you must not dwell on them. It does not matter what thought comes into your mind as long as you don't entertain the thought. The moment a negative thought comes into your mind you must replace it with a positive one. When you dwell or hold on to a thought a strong thought form is created. If you release the thought quickly, it can not produce a lasting thought form. This will take mental discipline and practice.

We are born into the material world in order to master ourselves. Self mastery is completed when we have gained complete control of our thoughts. Most people are not aware that we can control our state of mind by our thoughts.

Mind Exercise:

The positive thought diet. This mind exercise called the positive thought diet, is one that you will do for an entire day. With just one day of mild effort, you can change your life. So, for one full day, change all your thoughts to positive creative thoughts. If a negative thought enters your mind, quickly notice it, and then quickly change it to a positive thought. If you see someone that stirs up negative thoughts, quickly notice it, and then quickly change it to a positive thought. If something happens that stirs up negative thoughts, quickly notice it, and then quickly change it to a positive thought. The goal here is to stop thinking negative thoughts and replace any negative thoughts with positive thoughts. All bad things that happen to us are attracted to us by our own negative thoughts. This one exercise by itself can have a profound impact on a persons life. Try this exercise everyday until you are able to do it for an entire day without having any negative thoughts. One day of mild effort, you can change your life. If you keep doing this daily, it will become a very good habit that will change your life. The goal here would be to have only positive thoughts each and everyday for the rest of your life.

Habits

It takes twenty one days to make or break a habit, good or bad. Habits allow us to function on automatic pilot, saving us from the need to think about situations before we respond. Habits, sometimes serve only to reinforce the difficult patterns in your life. If you keep doing what you have been doing, you will keep getting what you have been getting. We each have habitual patterns of thinking, feeling, and behaving that have been practiced for so long and have become so integrated into our lives that we are no longer conscious of them. Indeed, much of your life is lived unconsciously through a patterned set of habits, some dating from before you were able to speak. Sadly, most people never truly break their habits, no matter how hard they try. Year after year, they slip into the same patterns of thoughts, feelings, and behaviors. Modern times have become so complex, and is lived at such a fast pace, that we give over great chunks of our waking life to our unconscious. How we live, how we eat, how we work, and even how we relate to others. When we live too much through our unconscious patterns, we create unconscious lives. Most of us are failing by not doing, by letting things happen in our lives, instead of directing our lives and determining our own outcome. If we get caught up in the small day to day busy stuff, we could miss our chance to give the commitment needed to achieve the greater things in life. People who fail to achieve their real desires in life do so because they major in minor things, they put all their time and energy into the non important minor things.

Energy

The soul is life itself locally manifested. The soul is an individuation of the divine spirit which is all there is. The soul is universal life energy. The energy of universal life is often called the spirit or soul.

How energy works. Everything is composed of vibration and resonance. These two components make up all things. A rock has a slow vibration and mammals have a faster or higher vibration. Resonance is like a vibrational quality or sound and this is how we respond to our environment, and the things in it. Mass and energy are interchangeable. The most important consequence of this is that mass is nothing but a form of energy. So, everything is a form of energy. The entire body is an electromagnetic field. This field can be altered with energy. This means that energy can exist as either solid matter or non solid matter, such as a beam of light. Energy is all around us, everywhere in all different wavelengths and frequencies. Frequency is how fast or slow something vibrates. The higher the frequency the faster it vibrates. Energy is also produced by our bodies from the food and liquids we ingest, "We are what we eat". When we speak, our voice saying words has released sound waves of energy causing ripples in the air around us. When we think, our brains release wavelengths of energy. Thought is a powerful energy in the universe. With thought we can do anything energetically! Our bodies are transmitters of energy and receiving stations for energy. We are made up of a multi-body system, not just the physical body, we called these bodies maya koshas or kosha for short. When we think thoughts, these non solid forms of energy go out into our multi-body system and greatly affect us. We can have energy patterns stored from events that happened yesterday as well as from many years ago or many lifetimes ago. Some of these patterns will be happy memories and some of them will be unpleasant and painful memories of something that happened to us. Disease is a manifestation of unbalanced energy. Disease is caused by some kind of imbalance, or by a problem with energy in a particular area, either too much or too little, or a blockage in its circulation. Healing then is a way of balancing energy. Throughout our lives we pick up negative forms of energy, such as fear, doubt, anger, judgment, criticism, blame, and others. Negative energy can also be directed at us from other people (consciously or unconsciously).

We are energy beings, we are that energy. Human beings operate within a magnetic field. The human brain is both a broadcasting and a receiving station for vibrations of thought. Learn to control your thoughts, for thought is energy. Mental images are concentrated energy. If you don't want it, don't think it. All forms of nature are merely energy in different illusory manifestations.

Your body is vibrating at a certain level. If you let your energy get to low your body suffers. This is the relationship between stress and disease. Love is the way we keep our vibration and energy up. It keeps us healthy. Anger, fear, and hatred are low energies that weaken you. Love and compassion are high energies that strengthen you. When one can learn how to direct his energy into wholesome channels instead of letting it stagnate in a pool of unfulfilled desires, they can accomplish anything. Man should strive gradually to redirect his energies upward from matter to spirit. Because you identify with your body, you think you need a form, however energy is formless.

A portion of your thought vibration affects the mind of other people, known as induction or telepathy. You can deliberately uplift the vibrations of those around you by elevating and radiating your positive thoughts. You can also change the vibrations of material objects to attract them into your life, or to fix broken things, or release anything that's unwanted.

Positive Energy

The goal is to get you to a place in your life where you are constantly in a positive state of mind, therefore constantly projecting positive energy. This positive energy will attract positive situations, people, and experiences into your life, often known as success and abundance.

We have a choice in life of either expanding or contracting our power. Anything positive, creative, or filled with love is expanding your energy, anything negative, destructive, or filled with hate and anger is contracting your energy. Often we choose to contract or depress our creative energy, and we become afraid to take action. We always have the power of choice. We can expand, or we can contract. We can expand and radiate positive energy, or we can contract and collapse on ourselves, whether we call that contraction fear, hate, or anger.

Vibrations

The three levels or planes of existence are physical, mental, and spiritual. Each plane vibrates at different rates, and these vibrational differences are the only distinguishing factors between planes. The higher spiritual planes vibrate the fastest, and the lower material planes vibrate the slowest, which is why matter appears dense and solid. Each plane is divided into subcategories and is subdivided from lower to higher vibrations. The universe is in constant motion at different vibrations. The only variable separating one plane from another is its vibration. The higher the vibrational rate, the higher the plane.

All matter is formed out of one primordial universal substance called "Ether". This ether spreading throughout limitless space is a universal medium, through which it is possible to convey force by means of vibrations. Ether fills the boundless space of the universe. It is the medium of conveyance for all known forms of vibration such as light, sound, heat, thought, etc. Ether is an infinitely subtle fluid, pervading all space. Ether forms a connecting link between all modes of substance whether visible or invisible, in all worlds, and may therefore be called the universal medium. Waves are set up in this medium by an impulse which generates from some particular point. This impulse might well be the desire or will of the spiritual being, that thinking, inner most essence of ourselves. We must accept the idea of thought as the initial impulse, which starts trains of waves in the universal medium. We must learn to make the impulses we send forth intelligent, well defined, and directed to some useful purpose. The waves spread all around just as ripples in a pond.

You are a vibration being. Every thought that you give your attention to expands and becomes part of your vibrational mix. Your attention to it invites it into your experience. This is an attraction based universe. Fear, guilt, anger, and other characteristics of ego effect our vibration and what we radiate. Allowing is simply the absence of negative vibrations and doubt is a negative vibration. A negative vibration will delete and cancel the positive vibration of your desire. Every thought, emotion, and desire vibrates and attracts experiences of matching vibration. If you'd like to attract better experiences, you must elevate your thoughts and emotions thus raising your vibration.

If we accustom our mental bodies to a certain type of vibration they learn to reproduce it easily and readily. If we let ourselves think a certain kind of thought today, it will be easier to think that same thought tomorrow. If a man allows himself to begin to think evil of others, it soon becomes easy to think more evil of them and difficult to think any good of them. It is clear therefore that we must exercise the greatest care as to what thought or emotion we permit to arise within ourselves. We must get into the habit of good thoughts. This is where we get the saying: "As a man thinketh in his heart, so is he". We are what we think. Another saying is "As above, so below".

The universe which is responding to the thoughts that you are thinking, does not distinguish between a thought brought about by your observation of some reality you have witnessed and a thought brought about by your imagination. In either case, thought is the point of attraction. If you focus upon it long enough, it will become your reality. To know whether you are sending out a positive or a negative vibration, simply take a look at the results you're getting in that area of your life. They are a perfect reflection of what you are vibrating. To raise your vibration simply means to give your desires more positive attention, positive thought, positive energy and focus.

If you want to find the secrets of the universe, think in terms of energy, frequency, and vibration. Those who study and practice the principle of vibration are using a higher law than physical law, thereby seeming to defy time and space to accomplish miracles. Nothing rests, everything moves, everything vibrates. He who understands the principle of vibration has grasped the scepter of power.

Law of Attraction

The law of attraction states that thought energy and projected energy attract similar energy. As a result we attract things into our lives accordingly. We attract into our lives whatever we direct our conscious attention to. Like attracts like. The law of attraction asserts that, on a vibrational level, like attracts like. You are a living magnet, you attract into your life people, situations, and circumstances that are in harmony with your dominant thoughts. You attract into your life whatever you give your attention and energy to, whether positive or negative. So when you give thoughts of hate, then others will give that back to you. When you give thoughts of love, others will give that back to you. Since the law of attraction is always responding to your thoughts, a deliberate focusing of your thought is important. So watch your thoughts as they create everything in your life. The law of attraction only responds to the vibration you are sending out right now. To reset, change your vibration. Just change the words you're using and the thoughts you are thinking. The law of attraction guarantees that whatever you are predominantly focused upon will flow into your experience. Life isn't happening to you, life is responding to you. You are the creator of your life. You are the writer of your life story.

Happiness

The power of happiness. True happiness is the ability to radiate positive energy regardless of external or internal circumstances. This ability to radiate happiness is independent both of how our life happens to be going and whatever emotional state we're experiencing. The greatest gift that you could ever give to another is your own happiness, for when you are in a state of love, joy, happiness, or appreciation, you are fully connected to the stream of pure, positive source energy that is truly who you are. The key to happiness is doing what you love with the people that you love. We can become happier by learning to direct our attention. We can choose whether to place our attention more on the positive or more on the negative. Happiness is a moment to moment practice, accessible at any time we choose. Happiness is power and power is being able to do what one chooses to do. Happiness is constantly passing us by because we are spending all our time pursuing it instead of being it. The only way to be happy is to be happy now. We may have many experiences and play a great variety of roles but the secret of true happiness lies in our ability to always know who we are, not the personality, the body, the mind, or karmic patterns. Meditation and self acceptance guarantees liberation. God wants us to live our dreams.

Path

A person on the spiritual path eventually attains salvation, that level of understanding and inward realization where he knows himself to be a soul which is but using mind and body for a purpose. If you want to be on a spiritual path, you must practice the presence of god at all times. Your life is sacred. There is and always has been a path for your soul, and if you follow that path, it will lead you to the inner utopia that your soul longs to experience in this lifetime. You have a duty to step into the greatest version of yourself. Integrity means living and acting in alignment with spiritual law and with the highest vision of yourself.

Inner World

Life is made of two realms, there is the inner world, and there is the outer world. Most of us only operate in the outer world, and don't even realize there is an inner world. We need to be connected to our inner world. Nothing is more fascinating than the journey of discovery into the world within. Everything that exists in the outer world begins in our inner most awareness.

Encased in the bodily prison, the soul consciousness and life force identifies with the physical vehicle and its mortal limitations. The trouble with most of us is that we live entirely in the outer world. We have no knowledge of that inner world which is responsible for all the conditions we meet and all the experiences we have. We have no concept of the spirit that is within us. The inner world promises us health, prosperity, happiness, and dominion over the outer world. This world is not the same to all people. Each one lives in his own domain. Peace and harmony may reign in one person's world, strife and war in another. But whatever be the circumstances of ones environment it consists of both an inner world and an outer world. The outside world is the one in which your life engages in action and interaction. The world inside determines your happiness or unhappiness. When you focus your attention within, you will feel a new power, a new strength, a new peace in body, mind, and spirit. Finding god within, you will find him without, in all people and all conditions.

Consciousness

Consciousness is a state of one's thoughts and feelings, an awareness of the individual's activity of the mind endowed with intelligence and energized with emotions. It is the universal energy from the vibrations of source, creator, or god source. It is an intelligence and guidance that transcends the dramas of the ego. (Ego is an aspect of one's personality).

Power flows from this universal higher source and we are connected to this power. It comes to us through feelings, emotions, and a detachment from the control of the ego desires. Higher consciousness is a higher awareness, a spiritual connection to a higher source. Accessing higher consciousness means that one transcends the normal busy mind of thought regarding the past, present, and future. Higher consciousness is the ever increasing awareness of one's spiritual essence, the meaning of life and the underlying spiritual nature of all things. Spiritual strength and wisdom flows into one's life offering inspiration, guidance, and all encompassing energy. Higher consciousness is one's deep feeling of connection to the cosmic universal force that cradles us in comfort, peace, joy, and bliss. How does one experience higher consciousness? For some, the accession of this mental and emotional awareness can be sudden and brief. For others, it is a matter of focused and deliberate concentration as in meditation, breath work, mind work, and energy work. When one functions at a higher consciousness, one is responsive to the guidance that is forthcoming. It is a calm knowingness which never fails in guiding us according to our highest and best good. Everything that requires mastery, be it health, finances, relationships, work, or over all harmony is done by raising our consciousness. By rising mentally or dwelling on your higher plane of consciousness, you escape the backwards swing of lower consciousness. Through an act of will, you can raise your mental vibrations above the lower plane of consciousness.

Our consciousness vibrates at a much higher wavelength than our bodies and is therefore out of range of the body's physical senses. We have to expand our minds and increase our vibrational rate. Mediation and some of the other exercises in this book will be very helpful with this. The level of consciousness you choose to tune into each moment of each day will determine the quality of your experience of the world. Everything in the universe is made up of energy and this energy vibrates at different frequencies. When you're vibrating in harmony with your souls highest emotions, you embark on an exhilarating ride to all that is good about life. You can live in heaven or you can suffer in hell. Heaven is divine consciousness. Being completely present to all that is and all that you are. Living by the soul is heaven, while being driven by the ego is hell. The mind made you is often called the ego.

When awareness is partially or completely removed from identification with mental processes, superconsciousness is experienced. Superconsciousness is a natural state to the soul. The reason many souls do not know this, is because their attention is identified with mental processes to the extent that they have forgotten their real, inner nature. Meditation is helpful because it helps us reconnect with our superconsciousness. Repeated superconscious episodes eventually purify the mental field, resulting in mental illumination and the removal of all delusions and illusions. Use of meditation techniques such as prayer, mantra, contemplation of inner light and or sound will enable us to remove attention from the outer sources of distraction and bring us to a place where spontaneous meditation can occur.

Additional Helpful Information – Vibrational States

You are a vibrational being. The law of attraction asserts that, on a vibrational level, like attracts like. You will attract people and things and events into your life based on your vibrational level. People who have a high vibrational state tend to pull into their lives people, things, and events that are also of a high vibrational nature. Likewise, people who have a low vibrational state tend to pull into their lives people, things, and events that are also of a low vibrational nature. Some people, things, and events can make you feel better. Some people, things, and events are neutral and will not change the way you feel. While some people, things, and events will make you feel worse.

If you find yourself in the presence of people, things, and events that are of a higher vibrational state than yourself, their higher vibration will raise your vibration and pull you up to a higher vibrational state. This will often cause you to feel better, have more energy, and have an improved attitude and outlook on life. This explains why people feel enlightened or inspired when they are in the presence of a very spiritual or holy person. If you find yourself in a situation where you are with people, things, and events that are of a higher vibrational state, I would suggest you spend some time there and enjoy the raised vibrational state.

If you find yourself in the presence of people, things, and events that are of a lower vibrational state than yourself, their lower vibration will lower your vibration and pull you down to a lower vibrational state. This will often cause you to not feel so good, have less energy, have an declining attitude about things, and a declining outlook on life. If you find yourself in a situation where you are with people, things, and events that are of a lower vibrational state, I would suggest you leave this situation as soon as possible, take your exit and run away as fast as possible. Sometimes people of a lower vibrational state will sense your higher vibration, and they will try to hang around you so they can suck that energy from you. Which will make them feel better and you feel worst. So, if you find yourself feeling drained of your energy I would suggest you leave as soon as possible.

You can tell a persons vibrational state by what they say and the way they behave. A person who says things of a positive nature and has a good outlook and does things to help people, is most likely a person of a higher vibrational state. Someone who is angry, or always complaining, and who likes to hurt people or destroy property, is a person of a lower vibrational state.

When you spend time around people of a lower vibrational level, like friends or family, you tend to pick up their negative or lower vibrational habits and spoken phrases, the things or phrases they say. This can be a problem, as doing so will result in lowering your vibrational state. I know a person who is always saying silly things like "Whatever", or "Oh well", or "These things happen", and other foolish things, and occasionally I catch myself using one of their phrases, and then I realize I have picked up one of their bad habits and have to watch myself so I do not start using these phrases and lower my vibrational state.

People who are not honest and tell lies are generally of a lower vibrational state. I know a person who lies all the time, about every stupid little thing, and to everyone, even when its not necessary. I find it difficult to be around this person when they are telling lies. When they lie to me, I can feel my vibrational level drop and my energy decrease. Remember telling lies creates negative thought forms, so don't do it. People with excessive drug and alcohol problems tend to lie a great deal. People with excessive drugs and alcohol usage are also of a very low vibrational level. Drugs and alcohol tend to lower a person vibrational state and thus are harmful to spiritual growth and advancement.

Another interesting thing I have noticed is when a persons vibrational level is to far apart from another persons vibrational level, for instance when a very high vibrational person comes into contact with a very low vibrational person, both parties usually experience a feeling of irritation or dislike toward the other person. This is due to the fact that the vibrational levels are to far apart. We are usually most comfortable around people who have a similar or matching vibrational level. I have a friend that I see once in a while who sometimes can be at a very low vibrational level, and when they are, I usually can tell as I feel irritation towards them. So when this happens I just keep my distance from this person so they do not lower my vibrational level. The funny thing is that as soon as they leave I usually feel a sense of relief and I feel better.

We all have times when there are changes in our vibrational level. When your vibrational level goes up, well that's a good thing, try to hold that higher vibrational level for as long as you can. When your vibrational level goes down, you need to do whatever you can to raise your vibrational level back up again. There will be some exercises later in this book that will help with this. One of your goals for life should be to raise your vibrational level and keep it at that higher level. Remember the law of attraction, like attracts like. So with a higher vibrational level, you will attract better people, places, and things into your life, or maybe I should say more success and abundance.

I once went into a movie theater and while waiting for the movie to start I noticed it was very loud and noisy. I started to feel agitated and noticed everyone else was agitated. So I decided to try something, I filled myself with light and love thus raising my vibration, then I projected it outward. A funny thing happened, after a few minutes the theater became quiet and it felt peaceful. Everyone had calmed down and it stayed like that throughout the movie.

In summary, your being will try to match the vibrational level of those around you, this can raise you up or pull you down. A person of a higher vibrational state will raise the vibration level of a person of a lower vibrational state. A person of a lower vibrational state will lower the vibration level of a person of a higher vibrational state. If you are with someone of a higher vibrational state they will raise you up, and if you are with someone of a lower vibrational state they will pull you down. This often happens in relationships. You start dating someone who is always bright and happy, and has a good outlook on life. You soon find that you are also become more bright and more happy, and your outlook is also improving. On the other hand, if you start dating someone who is sad and depressed, or always angry, you will find yourself becoming sad and depressed, and more angry. This is why so many relationships fail. We pick people based on things like appearance, or someone who has a great body, or for sexual reasons. We do not take into consideration things like their vibrational state or level. It is best to be with people, things, and events that are on the same vibrational level as you, or at a higher vibrational state than yourself. This will make your relationship and your life better.

CHAPTER

In the Beginning

In the beginning one was pure. As soul, one came into this world not bringing along any excess baggage, but then they created a lower mind. When they ceased to monitor it, it began to out create them, and this became their downfall. This part of man which began to out create the soul in the beginning still does so today. Psychology calls it the subconscious mind, Christianity calls it the devil. Until man is aware of this and looks to soul as the prime creator, man will always lean upon something else to do for him and will be its effect. One must set out to break the fixed desires of his own nature. These desires have been established in the subconscious mind over a period of many incarnations.

Time

Thinking fragments reality, it cuts it up into bits and pieces called time. The division of time into past and future is mind made. Past and future are thought forms and do not exist. Only the now or present exists. The essential self is eternal, it never changes. It is pure consciousness, and pure consciousness is timeless. Our normal experience of the passing of time is derived from change, the cycle of day and night, and the passing of thoughts. In deep meditation, when all awareness of things has ceased and the mind is completely still, there is no experience of change, and nothing by which to mark the passing of time. Time as we know it disappears. There is simply now. The essential self is beyond time and space.

The impression that your consciousness exists at a particular place in the world is an illusion. Everything we experience in the world is an illusion. Everything we experience is a construct within consciousness.

Now

There is no time like the present. It is the fear of tomorrow and the regrets of yesterday that rob us of today. Yesterday is history, tomorrow is a mystery, but today is a gift, that is why it is called the present. The past can only be remembered and the future has not happened, when it does happen it is the now. So everything that is real, is in the now. Give your attention to the moment, live in the now. It's always now. Surrender to the now, stop thinking, or at least stop paying attention to your thoughts. We are to live in the joyous moment, having given up attitudes and feelings of lack of worth, guilt over past actions (real or imagined), regret, fear, and doubt. When your attention moves into the now there is an alertness, it is as if you were waking up from a dream, the dream of thought, the dream of past and future. When your attention moves into the now there is just this moment.

When you feel fear, put it aside, it means you are living in the past or future, not in the now, not in the present moment. Whenever you have a problem it involves something from the past or future. You keep your problems alive in the present mind by giving them your attention and energy. When you suffer, that's a good indication that you lost the now, that you are not in the present, not in the moment. Step out of the past and the future, step back into the now, the present. The trouble with us is that instead of living only in the present, we try to live in the past and future at the same time.

Focus your full attention on the here and now, not on the past or future. When you give your full attention to whoever or whatever you are interacting with, you take the past and future out of the equation. When you are doing something, your thoughts should be focused on what you are doing and nothing else. When you are doing nothing, your thoughts should be empty. Being in the here and now, the present, is the door to the kingdom of god. This will help transform your life and everything in it.

One day I was looking out the window and there were three deer standing in the front yard eating the grass. As I was watching the deer someone that I know had pulled into the parking lot with their car and walked up to the front door right past the three deer which were less than fifty feet from them. The deer just froze and watched as this person walked right by them. When this person entered the house, I said "Did you see the three deer?" They replied "No". So I said "How could you miss them, you almost stepped on them". They replied "Oh, I was busy planning my day and did not notice the deer". This person is clearly not in the now, not in the moment, not in the present. They are in their mind thinking about the future. I was talking to someone else the other day and they did not hear a word I said, so I asked "Where were you?" They replied, "Oh my mind was somewhere else". Here is a good example of someone who is not in the present moment, they are lost in their own mind.

Have you ever driven some place and when you arrived there, you realize you didn't remember the actual drive, or did you do something and then not realize that you did it. Well these are good indications that you are lost in the past or the future and not in the present moment. Most accidents are caused by not being in the now, or the moment. Things like stubbing your toe, banging your finger, walking into something, all the way up to things like a car accidents occur because the person is not in the now, not in the present moment. A person who is not in the now has their attention somewhere else like the past or the future, so no wonder this causes accidents. A person operating in the now, or the present moment would never have an accident because they would be aware of everything happening in this moment and they would move themselves out of the way, thus preventing the accident from ever happening.

I know a person who thinks multitasking is the greatest thing in the world and does this all the time. They are always trying to do four or five things at the same time. Multitasking is very bad as you are dispersed, your mind is dispersed, plus your thoughts and attention are scattered, and this leads to confusion. Again this person is not fully in the present moment. I have seem this person try and do four or five things at one time, and the results are not that good. They will attempt to cook dinner, set the table, empty the dish washer, do their laundry, and read a magazine all at the same time. Usually one or more things are not correct and suffer, for example, the table does not have all the correct dishes and silverware, the dishes and silverware are not always returned to their correct places in the cabinets and silverware drawers, one food item is often cold or burn due to their lack of attention on cooking, and the fact that they will wait for the laundry to finish before serving dinner also sometimes allows the food to get cold. The funny thing is that it takes this person twice as long to prepare dinner and clean up. So where is the savings? Clearly this person is dispersed, their attention is scattered, and they are not fully in the present moment. I find that when I am around this person and they are attempting to multitask, that I start to feel scattered and dispersed, so I have to leave the area when this happens to relieve this negative feeling. The more you put in your mind and the more you let your mind handle for you, the less control you have over the mind, and then the mind runs on it's own, this is the reason we got in trouble in the first place. Multitasking push's you deeper into a mind controlled existence. It is always best to do one thing at a time and give it one hundred percent of your attention, this way you are in control, you are in the present moment, and you are telling the mind what to do. This will give you far better results and you will complete it faster. It is better to do one thing well, instead of four things half way.

The buddhist have a practice called mindfulness. Mindfulness means observing, focusing your full attention on the here and now, not on the past or future. Focus a minute at a time, a thing at a time, on whatever catches our interest. This is what the Buddhists call living mindfully. Basically it means doing one thing at a time with your full attention on the one thing that you are doing. We will talk about mindfulness later in this chapter.

Present Moment Exercise:

This is an exercise to put you into present moment or the now. When the past is troubling you or the future is worrying you, or when you feel that you are not in the present moment. Sit still, clear your mind and put all of your attention on your body and hold it there. Just notice, be aware of, and feel the body. If your thoughts wander, just bring them back to your body. Putting your attention on your body will bring you into the current moment. Then feel the power, feel the love inside of yourself. Do this till you are in the now and you feel better. Please do this exercise now and use it in the future when you feel that you are not in the present moment, or if you feel like you are dispersed.

Future and Past

Future is the creation of a future illusion and the working toward that illusion to make it a reality. The division of time into past and future is mind made. Past and future are thought forms and do not exist. Only the now, the present exists. When you open to god, you can know all because you are all. You discover that the past, present, and future are all occurring now.

Possible futures exist like branches on a tree, most of us only see the path were on, but some people, the gifted ones, see those branches. Our future destiny is to actually take an individual part and be active in guiding the great work of evolution.

The past is who you once were. The past is not who you are, it is who you were. The past doesn't have to control our future. Giving up the past is the key to inner freedom. We must come to a point where we no longer let previous programming run our lives. To be most fully alive, you have to be dead to the past and not let the past trouble you anymore,

Past and future are nothing more then a bad habit of your mind. Let go of what happened yesterday and don't worry about tomorrow. Most people don't live in the now because they think of yesterday or tomorrow most of the time. While the past can inform you, and the future can inspire you, the moment of choice exists in the here and now. By relinquishing your obsession with the past and your fantasies about the future, you can tap into the power of the present and feel the force of love that resides inside of you. When you become present, in this moment, in the eternal state of now, you will feel a level of peace, relaxation, love, and contentment that can only be accessed in this moment, it is called the precious present because when you are in it, it is the greatest gift you will ever give yourself.

Ego

Living by the soul is heaven, while being driven by the ego is hell. The mind made me is often called the ego. Ego is mistaken self identity because of intellectual error and the veiling or clouding of awareness that causes an illusional sense of being separate from god. Inaccurate self perception is the basis of egoism. The soul then presuming itself to be separated from its origins, identifies with this fragmented state of awareness. Egoism is the condition of being egocentric. Egoism is an extreme or exaggerated sense of self importance often characterized by arrogance and self centered willfulness. When this misperception is corrected, the soul, while aware of being individualized, is not confined to or limited by this view point.

Become aware of your inner saboteur, by simply being aware and recognizing when your saboteur is taking over, you can then take charge and slam the door on this unwelcome visitor. We all have this inner saboteur, this inner voice that is telling you that you can not do something. Setting ego aside means setting memory aside. Your ego is regarded as your sense of unique individuality, quite simply, it is who you perceive yourself to be. It is also what separates you from identifying with universal consciousness. Some refer to this ego as the mind out of control. An example; someone does something like cutting in front of you while you are driving, the ego jumps in and you yell at this person and give them the finger. This is an ego response and usually this happens before you actually have time to think about the situation.

The ego will bombard your mind with thoughts about trivia, bills, traffic, relationships, conflicts, or other issues. It's important not to fight the ego and get angry with it. Anger gives the ego reality and power. In truth, it is nothing but a nightmarish illusion. If you have a fear based thought, simply notice it and then release it. You can breathe out the fearful thought and breath in a replacement thought of love and true power.

The ego wants to fill you with thoughts of the past and the future. To be aware of the thought stream is to step out of ego. To stop the inner dialog and allow the direct experience of our life to unfold moment by moment, is to become free. By giving your full attention to this moment, an intelligence far greater than the ego enters your life.

The ego swims against the current. The soul swims in the direction that life is moving in. At any time you have access to either of these realities and all the experiences and emotions they bring with them. Your are either being guided by your soul or driven by your ego, the choice is yours. Ego could mean "Edge God Out". When we edge god out, we get ego. When awareness is removed from ego identification, only pure consciousness remain.

Breath

There are traditions which state that you can reach enlightenment by doing nothing other than paying attention to your breath. After watching your breath for several days, you begin to pay close attention to your sensations. You realize very quickly that you are obsessed with cravings for things like food, or warmth, and all sorts of desires, as well as aversion to unpleasant things. Then you realize the impermanence of it all. In the practice of pramayama, progress develops from mental concentration, control, and the power to visualize. Concentration while breathing is important.

Breathing Exercise:

This breathing exercise is called "Observe your breath". This is the simplest of all breathing exercises. Just put your attention on your breath, without trying to influence it. Do not try to speed it up, slow it down, or change the rhythm, just observe it with your mind. You should breath in through the nostrils if possible and exhale through your mouth. When you attempt to observe your breath, you may find that your attention wanders, usually to thoughts and images. Every time you become aware that this is happening, just gently bring your attention back to you breath. The observe your breath exercise is one you can do informally, any time, while waiting in line, or sitting at a stoplight. Whatever you are doing, look at your breath without trying to influence it. It is a good way to take a little break from the normal flow of thoughts, images, and attention to external stimuli, putting your mind briefly in a neutral place. Make a practice of observing your breath for a few minutes a day. You can also lengthen this period as a form of meditation. Please do this breathing exercise everyday this week.

Meditation

By meditating, attention is removed from involvement with physical and mental processes. Through meditation, you free your body from slavery and acquire mastery over it. The human race has been a slave to its body all though the ages. You and every other man are slaves to your body senses until knowledge gives your mind mastery over them. Meditation can not be effectively performed until concentration is at least partially mastered. The mind then has been made one pointed, it is then directed to and dwells steadily on any object of which knowledge is desired. In communion with god, you acquire god awareness, which means cosmic consciousness, by forgetting body awareness, which means material sensing. Cosmic consciousness is a higher form of consciousness than that possessed by the ordinary man.

Meditation Exercise:

This is a walking meditation. In this meditation you will put your attention on your breath while you are walking. Breathing in, I feel calm, breathing out, I feel at ease. You put your present moment attention on your breath while you are walking. Focus on your breath. You can also count, breathe in "one", breathe out "one", breathe in "two", breathe out "two", then "three/three", then "four/four", until you arrive at ten, then we will count backwards, breathe in "nine", breathe out "nine", "eight/eight", back to "one", and repeat "one" to "ten" and back to "one", etc. You may find that your attention wanders, usually to thoughts and images. Every time you become aware that this is happening, just gently bring your attention back to you breath. Do this meditation for five or ten minutes everyday for a week.

Feelings and Emotions

An emotion is energy in motion. Nothing rests, everything moves, everything vibrates. Your state of being is the way you feel about yourself at any point in time. Self esteem is merely feeling good about yourself, and when you do so, you develop confidence. Self esteem is what you think about yourself.

Perfection in a human being means freedom from pain, suffering, doubt, and fear. Positive and negative emotions can not occupy the mind at the same time. One or the other must dominate. It is your responsibility to make sure that positive emotions constitute the dominating influence of your mind.

Feelings and Emotions Exercise:

Handling emotional storms. If you find there is not enough peace in your emotions, your perceptions, or your feelings, you should practice calming them. Breathing in, I calm my feelings, breathing out, I smile at my feelings. When you are feeling burdened by strong emotions, either sit down, or lay down. As you breathe, bring your attention to your navel and to the movement of your abdomen. Using abdominal breathing, your abdomen rises and falls, follow the movement. Do not think about anything. Do this for ten or fifteen minutes or until the emotional storm has passed. You are breathing the emotional storm away. A strong emotion is like a storm. It is essential to understand that an emotion is merely something that arises, remains for awhile, and then goes away. A storm comes in, it stays awhile, and then it moves away. At the critical moment, remember that you are much more than your emotions.

Many people have no idea how to face emotions, and they suffer because of it. A lot of people are like that, and they think the only way to put an end to their suffering is to use drugs and alcohol, or in extreme cases they kill themselves. Why do we have to die because of an emotion? You should not wait for emotions to appear before you begin practicing. So sit or lay down and practice mindfulness of the breath, using the movement of your abdomen as the object of your attention. If you do this exercise for twenty one days, ten minutes or fifteen minutes per day, then you will know how to practice this whenever a strong emotion or emotional storm comes up. After ten or fifteen minutes, the emotion will go away and you will be saved from the storm. If it does not go away after fifteen minutes, continue this exercise until it does go away. Sometimes it takes more than fifteen minutes for the storm to pass.

You should do this exercise now as a test to become familiar with it and then do this everyday for the next twenty one days. Also use this in the future whenever you feel like there is not enough peace in your emotions, your perceptions, or your feelings. So whenever you are having a negative emotional response or an emotional storm, this is a good exercise to use to calm your emotions, your perceptions, or your feelings. It will calm you and calm your emotions.

Mind

Through concentration, the mind, ego, intellect, and the sense consciousness are all absorbed and a state of undifferentiated consciousness prevails. This is the state in which supreme spirit is seen through superconsciousness, or cosmic consciousness. One who has experienced this sees the same world differently thereafter. Perception is the same but one's perspective changes. Fear, pain, suffering, and bondage lose their meaning because all types of bondage are caused by attachment stemming from desire. This creates detachment, all desires disappear and one experiences the freedom that a drop of water experiences after it merges into the ocean. The habit of concentration will by itself tend to strengthen the mind, so that it will readily exercise control and selection with regard to the thoughts it sends out and those that come in from outside. You have to concentrate on one idea at a time.

Concentration should be practiced very sparingly at first, and should never be carried to the point of brain fatigue. A few minutes at a time is enough for a beginner, with the time being lengthened gradually as the practice goes on. The beginner should often break off his concentration sufficiently to notice the state of his body, and if he finds it strained, tense, or rigid, he should at once relax it, when this has been done several times, the links of association will be broken and the body will remain calm and resting while the mind is concentrating. The problems with humans are we identify with the mind. Learn how to silence the endless chatter of words and thoughts that flow unceasingly through the normal human mind. When the mind becomes filled with thoughts, do not pay attention to them, do not listen to them. Intense focus, which is concentration, gives thought power, and you can get anything you want using the power of your mind. Thought needs emotion to make it happen. Emotion gives the idea energy.

Thoughts

The universe which is responding to the thoughts that you are thinking, does not distinguish between a thought brought about by your observation of some reality you have witnessed and a thought brought about by your imagination. In either case, thought equals point of attraction. If you focus upon it long enough, it will become your reality. Another way of helping the growth of the mind body is the practice of concentration, that is, the fixing of the mind on a point and holding it there firmly not allowing it to drift or wander. We should train ourselves in thinking steadily and consecutively, not allowing our minds to run suddenly from one thing to another, wasting our energy away over a large number of insignificant thoughts. By controlling our thoughts, we can control our attitudes. This is the single greatest asset because attitude determines action. If you change your thinking you can change your attitude. If you change your attitude you can change your outer experience, your life.

The condition of the individual mind is the result of the thoughts which have dominated that mind. Any person may assume a mental attitude which will attract or repel others. Any person may also voluntarily change the attitude of his or her mind to either attract or repel things. Every mind is continuously changing to the extent that the individual's philosophy and general habits of thought change the composition of his or her mind. The habit of concentration will by itself tend to strengthen the mind, so that it will readily exercise control and selection with regard to the thoughts you send out and the thoughts that you allow in from outside. The mind is the device used for focusing the faculty of concentration, or attention directed by will. Developing powers of concentration is equivalent to developing muscular strength. Anyone can do it, it merely takes practice.

If you find that you frequently entertain idle, useless thoughts, you may want to put your mental energies to better use. You can spend more time practicing your powers of concentration, or you can remove your attention from that thought, or banish it from your conscious awareness. When you are doing something, your thoughts should be focused on what you are doing and nothing else. When you are doing nothing, your thoughts should be empty.

Mind Exercise:

This mind exercise is called concentration. At the beginning of concentration two difficulties must be overcome. First, the disregard of impressions continually being thrown at the mind, and the tendency to, respond to these outside impressions must be resisted. Secondly, the mind itself must hold a single image, for a time, the object of concentration. It has to confine its attention to a single object, to fix itself on that. So, for this exercise I want you to select one thing, it could be an object like a chair, then place your attention on that one thing. Do not let your concentration, your attention, or your mind wander. Keep your concentration, your attention, and your focus on this one item or thing. See if you can do this for one minute. Then try to do it for two minutes on the same item or a different item. Next move on to three minutes, and see it you can get up to five minutes of keeping your attention and focus on one thing. This is not very easy to do, as your mind will always try to fill you with thoughts of anything other then what you are focused on, So working up to five minutes is a really good achievement. Your ability to focus upon a narrower subject brings forth more clarity, while your ability to focus upon many things at once brings confusion. This is another reason why multitasking is not a good practice. Try this several times a day until you can get up to five minutes of concentration on only one thing. Please do this mind exercise everyday this week.

Mindfulness

Mindfulness means observing, focus your full attention on the here and now, not on the past or future. Focus a minute at a time, a thing at a time, on whatever catches our interest. This is what the Buddhists call living mindfully. When you are holding a cup of coffee in your hand, do it while being one hundred percent there. When you sit, sit. When you stand, stand. Whatever you do, don't wobble. Once you make your choice, do it with all your spirit. It's better to make a mistake with the full force of your being, than to timidly avoid mistakes with a trembling spirit. Concentration is the practice of happiness. When you eat an apple, try to practice concentration. Eat it in such a way that pleasure, joy, and happiness are possible the whole time. If I am one hundred percent there, the apple reveals itself to me one hundred percent. To stop the mind, try mindful breathing. Do everything in a mindful state, meaning always put your attention and thought on what you are doing. Always be mindful, don't stay in your head. Being in the here and now, the present, is the door to the kingdom of god. This will help transform your life and everything in it.

Mindfulness is keeping one's consciousness alive to the present reality. One must practice right now in one's daily life. When you are walking, practice mindfulness, you practice by keeping this one thought alive, "I'm walking" or "I'm walking down the street". You keep this one thought alive while you are walking, also consider each step that you take. If you practice this, you will experience the walk or the walk down the street, thus enabling you to enter the world of reality. Always keep your attention focused on what you are doing at that moment.

Mindfulness Exercise:

One Mindfulness activity for five or ten minutes. In this exercise you will do one activity for five or ten minutes practicing mindfulness. Set aside five or ten minutes everyday to practice mindfulness. Do only one simple thing like sweeping the driveway or massaging your feet. The point is to do one thing and one thing only for a full five or ten minutes. Keep all of your attention on the one thing that you are doing and do nothing else. Also keep your mind on what you are doing and on nothing else. If your attention or mind wander, just gently bring them back to the activity that you are doing. This exercise will help you pull your attention out of the past and the future, keeping you in the present. Please do this mindfulness exercise everyday this week.

Energy

There is a network of energy that flows through all living things. Everything around us has energy. This energy forms the basis of the thing and radiates outward from all things, including ourselves. You can see the energy field hovering around everything. We are subject to the energy that we are consciously or unconsciously radiating or receiving.

The principle of vibration or resonance is the foundational basis of the universe, recognizing that all is energy or light. Universal laws function all the time, on the principle of vibration and alignment. You are broadcasting and receiving vibrations to and from the world around you on a constant basis. The vibrations are formed by your thoughts, emotions, and life experiences.

The electromagnetic vibrations you send out every second of every day are what brought, and continuing to bring, everything into your life, big or small, good or bad, everything. That unique vibrational resonance attracts to you the people, events, and life experiences that match your energy field. Simply, you attract the people, events, and experiences that match the vibrations you are sending out into the universe. Every thought, emotion, and desire vibrates and attracts experiences of matching vibration. If you'd like to attract better experiences, you must elevate your thoughts and emotions thus raising your vibration. You can control your mental state, and lift your vibrations to any level you choose. Every thought, emotion, desire, or mental state is accompanied by vibrations.

Energy Exercise:

How to see energy, or exercise to see energy. Please follow the steps below.

1. Hold both your hands up so you can see the sky behind them.
2. Lean back (optional) and touch the tips of your index fingers together.
3. Keep the blue sky in the background.
4. Now separate the tips about an inch and look at the area directly between them.
5. What do you see?
6. Take your eyes out of focus a little and move the tips closer, then further apart.
7. Both finger tips will go slightly blurry, and as this happens you will see something like strands of smoke stretching between the tips.
8. Next do your palms, etc. and see what kind of results you get.

Keep trying this exercise everyday until you are able to actually see the energy as mentioned above. This exercise may take some practice.

Additional Helpful Information – Six Things You Can Do

There are six additional things you can do to help you regain the connection to your spirit, regain control of your life, and take back control of your life. These six things are:

1. Go within daily
2. Exercise the body
3. Eat well
4. Seek spiritual inspiration for your soul
5. Get sufficient sleep
6. Avoid drugs and alcohol

Go Within Daily

To go within daily means to meditate daily. To take the time to look at the inner world and detach from the outer world. A withdrawing of your focus from the physical conscious world, and an allowing of your focus to align with the inner world. Meditation is a break from life, a time to forget the stresses and worries of life. Through meditation, man reaches the state wherein he is always calm, never restless, where motions cease, god begins. Be still and know that I am god. When we say be still and know that I am god, the be still means quiet the mind, stop the thoughts. Your whole body and entire being changes when you practice meditation regularly. Meditation opens wide all the closed doors of your body, mind, and soul to admit the surge of god's power.

Exercise the Body

Exercising the body is important as this reduces things like stress and keeps the body and mind calm. It is very helpful to have a calm body and mind when performing activities like meditation. We need to turn off the noise in your mind, turn off all the thoughts in your mind. These are what keep you out of the now and keep you from flowing. Physical exercise is one way of doing this, as the exercise puts your attention in the now. Playing sports or dancing will also accomplish the same thing due to the physical activity. When you experience something like a loss or pain or an upset, often there is a physical mass associated with that negative experience. This mass can feel like a large burden or weight hanging over you. There can also be a great many negative thoughts and thought forms associated with that experience. The excess mental noise or negative thoughts can drive you crazy. Physical exercise, playing sports, or dancing helps to push the weight or mass away, quiet down the thoughts and mental noise, and helps you to recover from that negative experience.

Many years ago when I was a much younger man, I was dating a woman whom I believed to be the love of my life. I could see myself with her for the rest of my life. We were out on a date one night and something happened that caused me to behave very badly. She became very upset about my behavior and we had a huge fight. The next few days were very painful for me as she continued to be angry about my behavior. After several days she broke off our relationship. I was heart broken and devastated as my bad behavior had caused her to break up with me. I felt guilt and anger at myself for my bad behavior. This huge upset had overwhelmed me. I felt as if a very large mass or weight had rolled in on me, like a black cloud was hanging over me. I could feel the mass and weight of this black cloud hanging over me. For the next three months it was hard to do anything. Even sleeping was painful as my dreams were filled with her. I had to do something. A couple of years earlier I had done some weight lifting with some friends of mine. So I went out and purchased a weight lifting set and began lifting weights everyday for one hour. Next I began meditating everyday for one hour. The exercise and the meditation really helped reduce my stress. Then I remembered reading somewhere about keeping your thoughts positive to improve your attitude and outlook, like the positive thought diet exercise that I had you do in the previous chapter. So everyday I did this positive thought diet exercise and I tried real hard to keep my thoughts as positive as possible. I also began reading spiritual books and listening to spiritual tapes. I was trying hard to turn myself from this very negative outlook I was experiencing, to a more positive outlook. I was seeking spiritual inspiration for my soul. Within two months of doing this, the weight and the black cloud had lifted, I looked better, and I felt much better as my outlook had become much more positive, and I was even sleeping much better. All my friends commented on how much better I looked and how improved my attitude had become. So in summary, the exercise, the meditation, the positive thought diet, and filling my head with positive spiritual information had cured me of this bad state and black cloud that I was under.

Eat Well

A healthy diet is very important to our health and well being. Eating good food and healthy food will greatly help your body. Processed food and junk food have many chemicals that are harmful to the body and the mind. There are literally thousands of artificial substances around that can enter a persons system, many of which are toxic, and many of which we eat. We live in a chemically oriented society. A healthy diet, taking vitamins, exercising, and not smoking or abusing drugs or alcohol will help you remain healthy. A healthy diet, minus the chemicals makes connecting to your spiritual side much easier.

Seek Spiritual Inspiration for Your Soul

If you wish to be a spiritual person and live a spiritual life, it is best to keep your thoughts filled with positive spiritual information. I would suggest reading spiritual books often. Listen to spiritual programs. Fill your head with spiritual thoughts, as we become what we think about. As I mentioned earlier, when I was under the black cloud of my broken relationship, I also began reading spiritual books and listening to spiritual tapes. I was trying hard to turn myself from this very negative outlook I was experiencing, to a more positive outlook. I was seeking spiritual inspiration for my soul. This greatly helped my outlook and attitude. In just two months, I had gone from a very negative state of being to a very positive state of being and it changed my life.

Get Sufficient Sleep

In your sleep state, your physical body rests and repairs itself. In dreams your emotional body carries out its wishes, fears, hopes, and fantasies. Your being returns to the world of light, a higher dimension, which some people perceive as heaven. The reason we go to sleep at night is so that we can put all our bodies in order after the exertions of being awake and active. When asleep, you effortlessly leave your waking physical reality to enter a multidimensional universe where all things are possible. In sleep you reconnect with your very essence as a spiritual being.

A persons body requires sufficient sleep every night. Lack of sufficient sleep can greatly affect our well being and our state of mind. For each person this is different. Some people do well on six hours of sleep and others need eight hours of sleep per day. Too much sleep can be as bad as too little, as it can make us lazy and lacking in energy. The bottom line is your body needs sufficient sleep, so please ensure that you give that to your body. When you do not have sufficient sleep your vibrational level drops, you will have less energy, and this tends to pull you deeper into the mind. Remember we are trying to get out of the mind, not deeper into the mind.

Avoid Drugs and Alcohol

As mentioned earlier, a healthy diet, taking vitamins, exercising, and not smoking or abusing drugs or alcohol will help you remain healthy. Mental noise causes people to seek relief by using things like sex, alcohol, and drugs. Drugs and alcohol are very harmful to the body, mind, and our spiritual growth.

In the earlier story "Many Years Ago" I mentioned, the mind had gained control, or should we say the beings had lost control of the mind. Some refer to this as the ego, the mind out of control. Some beings had such a difficult time with this that they turned to things like sex, alcohol, and drugs in an attempt to quiet their mind.

People have used drugs and alcohol for as long as they have tried to ease pain and avoid problems. People often turn to drugs and alcohol as a solution to their problems. The problem, however, is not gone, but only masked by drugs and alcohol. The drug only masks the symptoms, it does not actually fix or cure anything. Drugs are essentially poisons and take their toll on a person's body by eating up its store of vitamins and minerals. In a drug ridden world, the person often finds himself victimized by the harmful effects of drugs and alcohol, even if taken years before. It is a proven fact that drug residues can be trapped in the body, and years later these residues can dislodge and affect the person again. A person's awareness, ability, and attitudes can be adversely affected.

People with excessive drug and alcohol usage are operating at a very low vibrational level. Drugs and alcohol tend to lower a persons vibrational state, they pull us deeper into the mind, and thus are harmful to spiritual growth and advancement. Drugs and alcohol have a huge negative impact on our spiritual growth as they dull our senses and impair our ability to connect with our spiritual side. Drugs and alcohol pull us deeper into the material world, pull us deeper into our minds, and further from the spiritual world. Remember as I just mentioned, we are trying to get out of the mind, not deeper into the mind.

If you are experiencing pain, or having problems, please try some of the exercises in this book to relieve the pain or problem. They are a much better solution to the pain or problem then drugs and alcohol are. If you have an actual physical or medical problem, you should always seek the help of a medical professional.

CHAPTER

New Country Within Us

To discover the new country within us we must first learn how to leave the old one behind. When death approaches we may look back upon this life and realize it was just a dream, our entire life was just a kind of dream. Kind of like the dreams we have at night. Then the goal of life would be to wake up from this dream. When we are awakened within the dream, the ego earth drama comes to an end. This is what I call the new country within us. To awaken from within the dream is our purpose now. So, awaken from the dream.

One of the things that happens as we grow older is we lose our spirit of play, our sense of play, our sense of having fun. We must recapture this spirit of play for it keeps us young. When you have the spirit of play, you feel alive, and everything and everyone around you senses this in you. The world is at your call and will do whatever you desire. Children have this, but we lose it as we grow older. We need to rediscover this spirit of play.

Realization

There is nothing wrong with being who you are, so there is nothing wrong with you. This means, you must change the way you look at things or your perception of reality. We should try to bring our realizations through into practical application in this world, and in this way we transform our lives and the lives of others. Possible futures exist like branches on a tree, most of us only see the path were on, but some people, the gifted ones, see those branches.

Can you really attract good luck, it is possible. Trying to change outer experiences before changing your inner beliefs is a total waste of time and energy. You must change your attitude and your beliefs first. Lucky people are often guided by intuition and hunches. By believing in yourself and your ability to attract good luck, you will set up a new momentum that will change and amaze you. The stronger your belief, the greater the success, but you have to desire it and act on it, not just wish for it. The greater your desire and willingness to act, the greater the power you have over life. It requires an unwavering belief that you are already lucky. Lucky people get lucky breaks.

Acceptance

You should accept the current conditions in your life. This does not mean that you can not change the current conditions, it only means accept what is in front of you now. Accept these conditions and be happy in them and with them, then you can move on to better things. In regard to others, you should allow others to be that which they want to be, and you should not pay to much attention to them, just let them be. We must learn to accept others the way they are. If you do not like the way they are, just don't spend any time with them. It is not your duty to try and change someone else, they will seek help and change when they are ready. The only person you really need to try and change is yourself.

Follow Your Heart

Do what you love, follow your heart's direction and the path to fulfillment in life will naturally unfold before you. Do not worry about making a living, true masters are those who have chosen to make a life, rather than a living. Do whatever you love and do nothing else. You have so little time, and how can you think of wasting a moment doing something for a living that you don't like to do, that is not a living, that is dying. Your longing is your calling. No matter what it is, if you go with it, you'll be guided, guarded, and assured success. When a purpose or path is laid before you, you have the choice to just trust and let it flow, or remain stuck in fear. Trusting the perfection that resides within you is the key. Remember, the universe loves you and wants you to succeed at everything that you do.

A big change occurred for me when I started to live life on my own terms, instead of someone else's terms. I now live life to the fullest and don't worry about what others think. I have determined what my values are and what I want most in life, and have aligned myself with those values and desires. Life is short and sweet, so make the best of it now. You can decide what you want and how you want to live your life. It's your choice, for it can be a wonderful life and you can create and have whatever life you want. Though no one can go back and make a brand new start, anyone can start from now and make a brand new ending. How many people dare to live the life they dream of?

Peace

Nothing has to be achieved in order to be at peace, all we have to do is stop doing, stop wanting things to be different, stop worrying, stop getting upset when things don't go as we wish, or when people don't behave as we think they should. People are disturbed not by things, but by the view they take of them. To experience the peace of your soul, you most enter a state of consciousness in which you are unattached to the past, present, or future. Here you will allow life to be and find peace.

Belief

We tend to think that our beliefs result from our experiences. We think that we believe the way we do because we have seen evidence to support those beliefs. But in truth the process works in the reverse order. First come the beliefs, then perception of reality in accordance with those beliefs. You perceive reality the way you do because of your beliefs. We ourselves are the key. Our minds are the tool with which we shape our perceptions and attract our experiences. So long as we believe the power is in the external world, we are indeed powerless to effect change. But once we accept the power that is rightfully ours, all things are possible. According to your faith be it on to you. This means, what you believe creates your reality and experiences.

Your beliefs influence the choices you make. Your beliefs set into motion inner processes and behaviors that influence how you move, act, and feel. What you believe, you receive. You must overcome negative beliefs that hold you back. Our capabilities and limitations are greatly influenced by what we believe, by our personal attitudes. Our abilities, potentials, and effectiveness are all affected by mental energy patterns. Take individuals who are convinced that they are incapable of comprehending some subject. The same thing often happens with powers of creativity. Everyone has immense potentials for creativity. Many people, however, repeatedly tell themselves that they could never learn to play music, or paint that picture, or write that book. Such things are true only if we believe they are true. We are fully capable of limiting ourselves by beliefs that have restrictive mental energies. People unnecessarily limit themselves by adopting limiting beliefs. Whether such beliefs come from others or we create them, we make them come true by adhering to them. It is just as easy, if not easier, to adopt and reinforce positive mental energy patterns. You can believe in your creative abilities, in your own worth, in your intelligence, and ability to learn, and these can become just as self fulfilling as negative beliefs. Belief in limitation is the one and only thing that causes limitation. Doubt paralyzes us and leads to mistakes and inaction. Doubt freezes the will and makes a person ineffective. When your mind is in doubt, you must turn your thought toward the divine force. Henry Ford once said "Whether you think you can, or you think you can't, you're right".

People often complain about their situation in life and maintain that they can do nothing about it. This portrays a belief in being powerless. Their belief system is the only thing preventing such people from making changes in their life situations. That can be a powerful obstacle. Your day to day beliefs, attitudes, thoughts, and feelings produce the energy patterns around which a majority of your physical experiences form, and of course any belief, limiting or otherwise, may be altered. Your beliefs affect the outcome of your life. Your beliefs, true, or untrue, form your world. What you imagine and feel to be true creates your life, because that is what your giving to the law of attraction, and that is what will be returned to you. Your imagination is more real than the world you see, because the world you see comes from what you imagine and believe.

The law of expectation. Before something can happen, you have to believe you can do it and that it will happen. Confidence in the power of the spirit in response to our desires and reliance on the world. This is what the bible calls faith. Faith is to believe that which you do not yet see and the reward of this faith is to see that which you believe. Faith is giving substance to things not yet seen. Faith is belief, nothing can be accomplished without it. Everything is possible for the person who believes. Believing is seeing. Anything is possible if you believe it.

Making Assumptions and Maybes

I need to talk about making assumptions and maybe's. One should never draw a conclusion about something without first gathering all the necessary facts about that thing. To not do so is guessing, this is the problem with assumptions. This is to draw a conclusion without the facts. The odds of being correct are very small. Assumptions lead to a maybe. A maybe is a state of uncertainty. This puts you in a state of confusion, mystery, and unknown. Confusion, mystery, and unknown states are lower vibrational states. This will cause you to lower your vibrational level. If you are not sure about something, don't guess, don't assume, just gather the facts. When the facts are present you will be in a state of certainty, you will know the truth, this is a higher vibrational state. Do you want to base your beliefs and conclusions on facts that are not true or correct? It is always best to base your beliefs and conclusions on facts that are true and correct.

Truth and Lying

When dealing with people, it is always best to be truthful. The truth can never come back and hurt you. If you can not tell the truth, or if you don't have anything nice to say, it is best to say nothing. If someone pushes the issue just say "I can not talk about that at this time".

Lying is a very dangerous and low vibrational activity and should be avoided at all cost. This is a negative energy exchange. To lie about things is to lower your vibrational level. Lying is also harmful to the people you are lying to, as it is a negative energy exchange, and an attempt to lower their vibrational level in addition to your own. People who are not honest and tell lies are generally in a lower vibrational state. I know a person who lies all the time, about every stupid little thing, and to everyone. I think this person has some type of automatic programming running in their mind that makes them lie, as often they lie so quickly that they have not even had time to think about and formulate a statement. Sadly, I don't even think they realize they are doing it. Clearly this is a person with a mind that is out of control and is running on automatic pilot. I find it difficult to be around this person when they lie due to the vibrational and energy decrease. When they lie to me, I can feel my vibrational level drop and my energy decrease, and then I just want to move away from this person and not be around them. Remember telling lies creates negative thoughts and thought forms, so don't do it. So, as I mentioned you should never lie, and if you can not tell the truth, or if you don't have anything nice to say, it is best to say nothing, or say "I can not talk about that at this time".

Secrets

Secrets are also a lower vibrational activity and should be avoided. Secrets lead to lies. To keep a secret you often have to lie. I know people who think everything relating to their life is a big secret. One person I know, always asks me about my life, but never tells me anything about their own life. For some reason this person thinks they should know what is going on in everyone else's life, but that their life is not anyone's business. This same person will tell me something about someone else and then say, don't tell anyone, trying to get me to keep secrets, which means they are trying to lower my vibrational level. Also, in order for me to keep the secret I will most likely have to lie to someone. Now, when this person tries to tell me a secret, I just say "Please don't tell me". Remember, if you can not tell the truth, or if you don't have anything nice to say, it is best to say nothing, or say "I can not talk about that at this time". The whole topics of secrets is a negative or lower vibrational activity. If you know someone who is big on secrets, they are in a lower vibrational state, and it is best not to have to much contact with them.

Thank You and Sorry

Another important concept is saying "Thank You" and "Sorry". When someone does something for you, you should always thank them, this is a positive energy exchange and a higher vibrational exchange. One should always incorporate gratitude and thankfulness into your everyday life. You should be grateful for the things you have and the things you want. Gratitude is an expression of love. When you feel grateful you are giving love. Say "Thank You" often.

When you do something to harm someone else, even if you did not intend to harm them, you should apologize and let the person know how sorry you are. By letting the other person know that you are sorry for your words or actions that harmed them, you are turning a lower vibrational exchange into a higher vibrational exchange. This will also prevent any future bad feelings that could lead to a future negative energy exchange. The two simple words "I'm Sorry" can make a world of difference. I have a relative who has done things to me that I would consider less then nice, and I have even mentioned to this person how much I disliked what they did and how much trouble it caused me, and you know they have never once apologized or said they were sorry, instead the reply was something silly like "Oh well" or "These things happen", as if saying "Oh well" or "These things happen" will make up for the things they have done. Clearly this person can not take responsibility for their actions, or even acknowledge what they did, or that they did something wrong. This has caused me not to trust this person, not to want to be near this person, and sometimes I get very uncomfortable when they are around. I have come to realize that they are operating at a lower vibrational state, and "Oh well" and "These things happen" is the best they can do from their vibrational level.

Talking and Listening

Another important topic is communication with others, or should I say talking to others and listening to others.

Most of us are so busy in our minds, that we don't really hear what other people say to us. When someone is talking to you, it is very important to stop what you are doing and pay attention or should I say put your attention on the person talking to you and listen to what they are saying to you. I talk to many people and it always surprises me how many people do not really listen. The effect of not listening or paying attention to the speaker, is that you are causing the speakers vibrational level to go lower due to your lack of interest. When you lower their vibrational level you also indirectly lower your own vibrational level, not to mention the speakers feelings toward you will decline and they may not wish to have further communication with you. When you put your attention on the speaker you actually raise the vibrational level of the speaker and yourself making for better communication and improved feelings between the two of you. I was talking to someone the other day and they did not hear a word I said, so I asked "Where were you?" They replied, "Yes I know you were talking to me, but my mind was somewhere else". Here is a good example of someone who is not in the present moment, they are lost in their own mind.

The same holds true when you are speaking to someone. When you are talking to someone it is very important to stop what you are doing and pay attention or should I say put your attention on the person you are talking to. The effect of not paying attention to the person you are speaking to is that they will not have an interest in what you are saying, causing your vibrational level to go lower due to their lack of interest.

When you lower your vibrational level you also indirectly lower their vibrational level. This will cause feelings to decline for both parties. When you put your attention on the person you are speaking to, you actually raise the vibrational level of both parties, making for better communication and improved feelings between the two of you.

What you say is also very important. If you speak to others in a positive way you are raising the vibrational level of both parties. When you wish to get people on your side or befriend them, you will always do better by raising the vibrational level between both parties. When you speak to others in a negative way, you are lowering the vibrational level of both parties, which can lead to bad feelings and other problems. The rule is, if you don't have anything nice to say, it is best to say nothing. The buddha called this right speech, if you cannot say something in such a way that the other person feels good on hearing it, then it is better to remain in noble silence. Think good, do good, speak the truth.

Breath

When you are depressed, the best thing to do is breathing and any kind of exercise or sport. It is more important to breath out than in. Pulling in the stomach and exhaling, empty the lungs thoroughly. Since nature hates a vacuum fresh air will then rush in.

Breathing Exercise:

This breathing exercise is called "Start with exhalation". In this exercise you are going to observe the breath again, but this time, starting with exhalation. Start by observing your breath, but begin each breath with the exhalation, so breathe out, breathe in, breathe out, and breathe in. Do this for five or ten minutes, simply observing your breath, without trying to influence it. By doing this exercise you are learning to take greater control of the breathing process, and to deepen breathing by increasing the amount of air that you move out. When you put your attention on the out breath, you will actually push out more air. The more air you move out, the more air you will take in. Do this exercise everyday this week.

Meditation

As you meditate, your lower self or ego may try to distract you. It does this because it is afraid that you will feel peace of mind. If you are centered in peacefulness and are unafraid, then the ego loses all of its power to control you with fear. The ego will bombard your mind with thoughts about trivia, bills, traffic, conflicts, your relationships, or other issues. It's important not to fight the ego and get angry with it. Anger gives the ego reality and power. In truth, it is nothing but a nightmarish illusion. So, if you have a fear based thought while meditating, simply notice it and then release it. You can breathe out the fearful thought and breath in a replacement though of love and true power. Meditation is best done in the morning when the body and mind are quiet. However, meditation can be done at anytime. Meditation is a break from life, a time to forget the stresses and worries of life.

A Mantra is that which enables our consciousness to become free from worldly thoughts and to go into a state of concentration. By the power of sound inherent in a mantra the mind becomes controlled and concentration becomes well established. The word mantra is sanskrit and may be translated as "Thoughts that liberate from the world of illusion". Mantras also refer to the science of mystic sound and vibration. Mantras are listened to or recited by a practitioner for many different purposes as a means of achieving different states of consciousness, or for creating resonance with specific attributes of divine energy.

Meditation Exercise:

For this meditation we will be using the spiritual eye often called the third eye. If you close your eyes, take a few deep breaths, and place your attention on the area between your two physical eyebrows, you will begin to see or feel an oval shaped object lying on its side, this is your spiritual eye or third eye. Try this now.

This is a Mantra meditation. Please do this meditation twice a day for the entire week, in the morning when you first get up and again in the evening. When awareness is partially or completely removed from identification with mental processes, superconsciousness is experienced. Superconsciousness is natural to the soul. The reason many souls do not know this, is because their attention is identified with mental processes to the extent that they have forgotten their real inner nature. Meditation is helpful because it helps us reconnect with our superconsciousness. Repeated superconscious occurrences eventually purify the mental field, resulting in mental illumination and the removal of all delusions and illusions. Use of meditation techniques such as prayer, mantra, contemplation of inner light and or sound will enable you to remove attention from outer sources of distraction and bring you to a place where spontaneous meditation can occur.

Meditation should be practiced daily. The easiest way to ensure regularity of practice is to meditate early in the morning, before thinking about the day's duties and projects. Ten to fifteen minute sessions will clear awareness, calm mental processes, reduce stress, calm the nervous system, strengthen the immune system, and enliven the systems of the body. When meditating for the purpose of experiencing refined conscious states, sit for a longer period of time. After practicing a meditation technique, rest in the tranquil silence for a short time before moving on to your next activity.

The easiest way to meditate is to listen to a mantra, a pleasant word or word phrase that will attract your attention and keep it focused. So, sit comfortably and upright, with your spine straight. Inhale more deeply than usual, then exhale. Do this two or three times. Relax and be still. With your eyes closed, look into the spiritual eye or third eye center, by concentrating at the spiritual eye center between the eyebrows. Be aware of your natural breathing rhythm. Mentally recite the mantra with inhalation or exhalation. The word "God" or "Love" or "Peace" can be used as a mantra. Pick the one you like the best. For this meditation mentally recite it when you exhale. As your body becomes relaxed, and thoughts and emotions are quieted, breathing will be slower, and thoughts and images will be less distracting. If your attention wanders, bring it back to the mantra. When your mind is quiet, disregard the mantra and rest in the peaceful silence for the duration of the meditation session. If thoughts, or random mental images interfere with concentration, or if you are too passive and only semiconscious, resume the use of the mantra until you are again alert and meditation flows smoothly.

The purpose of meditation practice is to calm subconscious impulses which cause thoughts and mental processes to occur. When awareness is clear and concentration is steady, superconsciousness devoid of thoughts and emotions will be experienced. Remember to allow inhalation and exhalation to occur naturally. Devotional prayer, breath awareness, and listening to a mantra, are all helpful to quiet the mind.

Feelings and Emotions

We need not be mentally or emotionally disturbed by memories of painful incidents, because they are only mental impressions of prior events and experiences. They can be dispassionately recalled and viewed, freeing attention, energy, and abilities for more meaningful purposes. When you are depressed, the best thing to do is breathing and any kind of exercise or sport. Deep breathing has a generally calming effect on the whole personality, reducing stress and nervous tension. Anger, resentment, and hatred are lower energies that weaken you. Love and compassion are higher energies that strengthen you. You have to see things in your current situation as you want them to be, not as they are now.

Past Problems

Past and future are nothing more then a bad habit of your mind. Concerns about the past or future are delusions. The past is who you once were. The past is not who you are, it is who you were. When you suffer, that's a good indication that you lost the now, you are not in the present, or the moment. Step out of the past and the future, step back into the now, the present. When you feel fear, put it aside, it means you are living in the past or future, not in the now, not in the present moment. The trouble with us is that instead of living only in the present, we try to live in the past and future at the same time.

The past doesn't have to control our future. Giving up the past is the key to inner freedom. We must come to a point where we no longer let previous programming run our lives. Whenever you have a problem it involves something past or future. You keep your problems alive in the present mind by giving them your attention and energy. Thoughts can carry a negative emotional charge like anxieties or old images we'd rather not think about. Thoughts seem to have the power to lift us up or bring us down, and sometimes jerk us around like puppets on a string.

The key to unlocking the mind entails remembering to bring our awareness back into the present moment, not the past or future. The mind likes to replay past situations and thoughts, and play possible future situations. The mind or mental noise can only relate to the past or the future. Past or future, that's where the mind lives, where it gets its power, where like a demon, it draws our attention out of the peace and sanity of the present moment.

Chinese philosophy links depression with thinking too much, so give yourself a break. Strive to be detached from desires and to remain indifferent to fame or personal gain. This is another ancient secret to preventing mental illness.

Feeling and Emotions Exercise:

Control your emotions through breathing. This is a second exercise to control your emotions. When your emotions trouble you, do the following exercise. Inhale slowly through your nose, mentally counting 1-2-3-4-5-6. Hold the breath mentally counting 1-2-3-4-5-6. Now exhale the breath slowly through your mouth, mentally counting 1-2-3-4-5-6. Keep your attention on your counting and your breath. Continue this exercise until your emotions subside. As a test, do this exercise for five to ten minutes everyday this week.

You know that good blood circulation is necessary for the well being of your body. The same is true for psyche, you must live and practice in such a way that your consciousness benefits from good circulation. Bad circulation of psychological elements creates problems.

Blocks of suffering, fear, jealousy, distress, and other negative emotions are stuck in the depths of your consciousness, they can recirculate, and make you feel the negative emotion again. That's why you have closed the door to your consciousness, because you do not want these things to come to the surface. You are afraid of the pain in you, and so whenever there is a gap in your day, you fill it up with things like sports or television so these blocks of suffering do not come up to the surface. In this way you create bad psychological circulation, and mental problems will soon appear. While you are sleeping, accumulations of suffering will reveal themselves to you in your dreams. Depression, fear, and confusion may also manifest in the body. You will have headaches and all kinds of other aches and pains. Buddhism teaches that the body and mind are two aspects of the same thing. The cells of your body are not only physical, they are also mental. They are both at the same time.

Mind

The mind is like a reflex organ, it reacts to everything. It fills your head with thousands of random thoughts everyday. People are not their thoughts, they think they are and it brings them all kinds of sadness.

Thoughts that come into your mind are not always your thoughts, sometimes they come from the people around you. That's why its good to find seclusion, like going out into nature by yourself to get away from the thoughts of others. You will find that while in seclusion your thoughts are very positive. The negative thoughts sometimes come from others. If you sit quietly and observe your mind, you will see that it is full of mixed signals.

The man who can control his thought can have what he wishes to have and do what he wishes to do, everything is his for the asking. Thought will always bring back to us what we send out. To those who do believe, it will come true in their lives. Without mental clearness on the part of the thinker there can be no real creative work done. You take control of your own life by taking control of your own thoughts.

One way to stay alert is to trick your mind by asking it questions, the secret is to keep asking your mind questions regularly. The more questions you can ask, the more you will be be control of your mind.

Your mind will be working with you and doing what you want it to do, instead of working against you. Periodically say to yourself, "What am I thinking, would I like this thought to create my life, would I like to have the experience that this thought could bring to me".

When one dwells in the positive mind, he is the master, when one dwells in the negative mind, he is the slave. The negative state of the subconscious mind is that of the slave. The goal of all spiritual seekers is to become stable in the positive state. When we change our thinking, we change our reality.

Thoughts

Often, when we want to make a change in our lives, the subconscious mind will replay our dysfunctional thoughts. These dysfunctional subconscious thoughts, and most of us have a large share, will sabotage our good intentions. The negative thoughts are just sitting there in the subconscious waiting for an opportunity to express themselves. We frequently hide our true greatness by staying in jobs, relationships, friendships, and habits that dim our light and diminish our spirit. You should live in the spirit of creation. You are the creator of your own reality and life can show up no other way for you then that way in which you think it will. You think it into being. Change your thoughts and your world will unfold in new and more positive ways.

Mind Exercise:

This mind exercise is called "Accurate observation". You should start small by looking at something like a photograph or picture, then remove the photograph or picture and see how much you can recall, see how many details you have observed. Do this several times until you are good at it. Then move on to something larger like a room. Walk into the room and look around for a minute, then leave the room and see how much you can recall, see how many details you have observed. Do this exercise several times daily for the entire week. Then in the future do this exercise periodically to keep your observation skills sharp.

Accurate observation, is definitely a faculty to be cultivated. Most people go through the world with their eyes half closed. Ask someone what we have observed while walking down the street. Many people will have observed next to nothing, others a few things, and some will have observed many things. It is said that Houdini trained his children in observing the contents of the shops they passed, while walking along the streets of London, until they could give the whole contents of a shop front which they had passed.

Mindfulness

Every day and every hour, one should practice mindfulness. Do everything, each task in a relaxed way, with all your attention. Enjoy and be one with your work. Live in the actual moment. Only this actual moment is life. Live each moment of everyday. We must live this moment in a deep way. Don't wait to start living. Your life should be real in this very moment. You can live every moment of everyday deeply, in touch with the wonders of life. If you are handling the present moment well, with all your wisdom and compassion, there is no need to worry about the future, because the future is made only of the present moment. Mindfulness is the miracle which can call back our dispersed mind and restore it to wholeness so that we can live each minute of life. Mindfulness itself is the life of awareness, the presence of mindfulness means the presence of life.

In a buddhist monastery, everyone learns to use breath as a tool to stop mental dispersion and to build up concentration power. Concentration power is the strength which comes from practicing mindfulness. It is the concentration which can help one obtain the great awakening. To master our breath is to be in control of our bodies and minds. Each time we find ourselves dispersed and find it difficult to gain control, the method of watching the breath should always be used. After about ten or fifteen minutes, your thoughts will have quieted down. You can also count your breath, see previous breathing exercises. In those moments when you are upset or dispersed and find it difficult to practice mindfulness, return to your breath. Your breath is the wondrous method of taking hold of your consciousness.

Of course, to take hold of our minds and calm our thoughts, we must also practice mindfulness of our feelings and perceptions. To take hold of your mind you must practice mindfulness of the mind. You must know how to observe and recognize the presence of every feeling and thought which arises in you. So what exactly should you be doing concerning such thoughts and feelings? Simply acknowledge their presence. For example, when a feeling of sadness arises, immediately recognize it "A feeling of sadness has just arisen in me". If the feeling of sadness continues, continue to recognize "A feeling of sadness is still in me". The essential thing is not to let any feeling or thought arise without recognizing it in mindfulness. Practice like this is to become mindful of your feelings and thoughts. You will soon arrive at taking hold of your mind. When we are angry, we ourselves are anger. When we are happy, we ourselves are happiness. When we have certain thoughts, we are those thoughts. We are both the mind and the observer of the mind. The most important thing is to be aware of the thought. The mind can only observe itself.

Mindfulness Exercise:

This mindfulness exercise is called the "Slow motion activity". I would like you to do this several times during the week. We will do a slow motion bath, please allow yourself thirty minutes to take a bath. Don't hurry for even one second. From the moment you step into the bath tub till the moment you step out of the bath tub, let every motion be light and slow, be attentive to every movement. You should take your time and do everything slower than normal, this way you can really experience the slow motion bath and enjoy it. Place your attention on every part of your body as you wash it. Follow your breath, be mindful of every action. The goal here is to be mindful in every action that you do, so when you are washing your foot, have all your attention on washing your foot, and do it slowly. Many people find this to be a very enjoyable experience, and continue to do this whenever they take a bath. When I take a bath, I always do the slow motion bath. If you do not have a bath tub, or you do not feel like taking a bath, you can do a slow motion body massage. Using the instructions from above, massage every part of your body slowly for thirty minutes.

Energy

When you remember an incident from the past, you are focusing energy. When you are imagining something that may occur in the future, you are focusing energy. And when you are observing something in the now, you are focusing energy. So no matter what you look at, you are focusing energy causing you to offer a vibration to match what you are looking at. So be careful at what you look at, as this is what you are attracting. We create our own reality by attracting to us magnetically the energy fields, people, and experiences which match the imagination of ourselves that we are broadcasting. To raise your vibration simply means to give your desire more positive attention, energy, and focus.

Energy Exercise:

Changing the energy of an experience. If there is an energy created by something you did or didn't do, something said or unsaid, change it now. Place your attention on that moment and experience the energy of that moment as it should have been. Continue to do this until it feels right. Pick any event past or present and do this for several minutes until it feels right. Use this exercise whenever you want to change the energy of an experience. This can be useful if you wish to change the energy of a past hurtful experience that keeps arising, or coming up in your mind. This will change any negative energy related to that experience to a positive energy and it should stop bothering you. Remember, experience the energy of that moment as it should have been. Do this exercise everyday this week.

Appreciation

If you want something, appreciate it. When you appreciate yourself, others, or the thing you want, you are offering no resistance. The more you maintain these good feeling thoughts, the higher your vibration, and the more the law of attraction will deliver to you the things you desire. This will also put you in a position to receive even clearer guidance from your inner source. The more you practice this, the less resistance you will have, and the better your life will be. I should mention, we are here to be happy and enjoy life. So anything that makes us feel bad goes against our inner being and should be avoided if possible.

Appreciation Exercise:

The appreciation game. Do this for five or ten minutes everyday this week. Look around and notice something that pleases you. Hold your attention on this while you consider how wonderful, beautiful, or useful it is, appreciate it. The longer you focus, the better you should feel. This will improve your mood and raise your vibration. This can also be used if you are not in a good mood, as this will improve your mood and raise your vibrational state. This is an exercise you should use whenever it is needed in the future.

Additional Helpful Information – Keep it Sweet and Friendly

This technique called "Keep it sweet and friendly" is useful when dealing with difficult people. When you encounter people who are grumpy, or complaining, or not easy to get along with, or who are trying to give you a difficult time, use a technique I call "Keep it sweet and friendly". Not everyone in this world is going to be friendly and nice. Remember, people at a lower vibrational level will try to start fights, say unkind things, or cause trouble and create problems for others, it is in the nature of a lower vibrational being. So when you encounter people who are not so friendly and nice, people of a lower vibrational level, it is best to engage them in conversation that is positive, sweet, light, and friendly. Say things like "What a nice day it is", or "You look nice today". If they say something negative to you, just reply with a sweet and friendly reply. If they say to you "you are dressed funny today", simply reply, "Yes I know, thank you. Isn't it a lovely day". Never defend yourself as this will just cause the person to want to say more unkind things to you. It is best just to give a sweet and kind reply and then go about your business, not engaging this person any further. Also, never say anything negative to this person, as this will cause the unfriendly person to want to attack you, or want to start trouble with you, and once this has started this person may wish to cause you problems every time they run into you. They may also start trouble for you behind your back. So, it is best to see these people for what they are, a person at a very low vibrational level, therefore keep it sweet and friendly so they have no reason to see you as a target. Remember, lower vibrational people are very much in their minds and we are attempting to get out of our minds, so do not let them pull you back into your mind, or back to their vibrational level.

I should mention, use this technique when you encounter people who are always complaining, or who always say negative things, or who are always talking bad of others. It is best not to engage in similar conversation with these people. To do so is a negative energy exchange and will lower your vibrational level. Remember these people are in a lower vibrational state. The only way to handle them is with the "Keep it sweet and friendly". And, if that does not work, it is best to leave and not engage in any further conversation.

CHAPTER

Awareness

The individual mind narrows our awareness down, as if we are looking at the world through a peep hole. Most people will never know anything beyond what they see with their own two physical eyes. They hypnotize themselves by listening to the thoughts in their head, so they're in a kind of trance, and they're not really aware of anything around them. Most people are lost in this trance, listening to the thoughts in their head. Outward thinking develops the physical qualities and desires of man, while inward thinking unfolds the spiritual qualities which have been waiting to unfold for the long ages of man's slow journey to the light of his own divinity. Do you wish to be conscious or unconscious, with awareness or lack of awareness, as the cause of your experience or as the effect of it. To be conscious and aware means to be at cause of your experience, to be unconscious with lack of awareness means to be at effect of your experience. Become self aware, aware that you are consciousness, that you have a consciousness, and become aware that you are. Through meditation, you free your body from slavery and acquire mastery over it. The human race has been a slave to its body all though the ages. You and every other man are slaves to your body senses until knowledge gives your mind mastery over them.

In communion with god, you acquire god awareness, which means cosmic consciousness, by forgetting body awareness, which means material sensing. Cosmic consciousness is a higher form of consciousness than that possessed by the ordinary man. In each communing with god you get a little more each time your soul touches the universal soul or god. When awareness is removed from ego identification, only pure consciousness remains. To restore our awareness to its original state we need to be able to discern the difference between our real pure conscious nature and the fragmented state of ordinary awareness commonly identified with thoughts, memories, emotions, and sensory perceptions. We can then engage in constructive actions that result in self discovery and enlightenment. Remember the universe is a continuum, a seamless manifestation of the energies of god's consciousness, and your state of consciousness, therefore actions influence everything in it. Awareness is how the human being experiences the light of consciousness. The more spiritually conscious you are, the more constructive are your influences as you awaken to the states of spiritual growth. All souls are benefited and planetary consciousness is refined by your enlightenment. You must become aware or your enlightenment, as you are already enlightened.

Separateness

All our troubles arise by thinking of ourselves as separated units, and then existing in our own mental space or state, thinking only of our separate interests, our separate goals, our separate joys and sorrows. All separateness is an illusion as all things are ultimately interconnected. Do not remain in the illusion that you are separate from the whole. When man rises, he then finds for the first time that separateness belongs only to the lower worlds, that he is one with all others, and that without losing self consciousness, his consciousness can expand to embrace the consciousness of all others. We need to break through the illusion of separateness.

Oneness – Inner Connected

There is a field of energy that connects all of creation. This field of energy connects everything. Everything is one, and we are part of the one. Everything in our world is connected to everything else. To tap the force of the universe itself, we must see ourselves as part of the world rather than separate from it. Become aware of your oneness with god. Feel your connection to the universe. You are the entire universe. The sun, moon, and stars revolve within you. You are in all and all is in you. Then you realize beyond all trace of doubt that the world is in you, and not you in the world.

The home of the soul is in the realm of the absolute where divine spirit dwells. Your soul is now living in the realm of the relative and is on a journey home, when it returns home it joins once again with the rest of itself. It reunites with divine spirit. We are specialized units of pure consciousness, functioning in the world through mind and body. Our mind is a unit of the cosmic mind or consciousness, god's mind or consciousness. Our body is made up of the ingredients of nature. Since we are units of pure consciousness, using a mind which is a unit of god's mind, and a body which is formed of ingredients of nature, which is god's energy in manifestation, we literally live in god all of the time. This only has to be consciously acknowledged, realized, and expressed. Problems are due to errors in understanding and perception. Remove the errors in understanding and perception, and the problems cease.

God

God, love is the essence of who you are. You don't need time to know who you are. You can only know yourself in the now, the present. To know who you truly are beyond mind and form, you need to enter the now. Become aware of your oneness with god. God dwells within you. When we recognize god as the source of all good, and are willing to trust in him, we begin to manifest a healthy condition in our bodies and in our external affairs. God talks to us all the time, but most of us do not listen. So, listen to the voice within, this is god talking to you. Intuition is soul guidance, appearing naturally in man during those instants when his mind is calm. The goal is to calm the mind, so you may hear the infallible counsel and guidance of the inner voice. Be still and know that I am god, means quiet the mind so you can go within and connect with your true self. If you do not go within, you will go without. There is nothing you can not be, there is nothing you can not do, and there is nothing you can not have when you are connected to your true self. Meditation is connecting with god for the purpose of working knowingly with god.

The soul, being an individualized unit, or aspect of god's consciousness, has within it all of the characteristics and capacities of god. Know the truth and the truth shall set you free. The truth of who you really are. God is the energy that you call life. God and life are the same thing. Life is energy. Souls are destined to awaken from the dream of mortality to full realization of god.

Progress on the Path

How can we know if we are making progress on the spiritual path. The degree of absence of thought is your measure of progress on your spiritual path. That doesn't give you much to think about (that's a joke). Unfortunately, no instruction manuals were provided when we came to this planet. The way you are is not the result of what has happened to you, it is the result of what you decide to keep inside you. All permanent and lasting change must come from the inside. If you were going to die in one year, what would you do? Make a list and do those things? All we have to do is decide what to do with the time that is given to us. This is very important, decide, it is our creation. We are the source of all in the material and spiritual worlds. Everything emanates from us. Contemplate ourselves as surrounded by the conditions which we want to produce. If you believe that you write the tale of your life, then the ending is also up to you.

Karma

The concept of karma is "Do unto others as you would have others do unto you". Karma is the belief that whatever energy and actions you exhibit will eventually return to you like a boomerang. In some cases, the effect will be immediate and in other cases it may take lifetimes to catch up with you. This is due to the law of attraction, what you do to others will be attracted back to you and will come back to you. When you believe in karma, the rules about right and wrong are no longer necessary. There is nothing that can work more powerfully to prevent human injustice than the belief that any unkind deed that you do will be countered by an unkind deed toward you, whether or not anyone is aware of the unkindness that you have committed. Likewise, if you do good deeds to and for others, good deeds will be returned to you. We are where we are in space and time, and our circumstances are what they are because of our habitual states of consciousness, mental states, choices, and personal behaviors. Considering the matter of fate, the law of cause and effect or karma, we should acknowledge that what we have experienced, thought, and done in the past has produced our present circumstances. We may have many experiences and play a great variety of roles, but the secret of true happiness lies in our ability to always know who we are, not the personality, the body, the mind, or karmic patterns. Meditation and self acceptance guarantees liberation. It has been said, "There is no fate, but what we make for ourselves".

Love

Our divine spiritual origin is love. Love is the source of all our power, of everything we need and desire. To block the awareness of love is to block everything. We have been taught to live in fear. Fear is the energy which contracts, closes in, closes down, hides, and harms. Love is the energy which expands, opens up, moves out, shares, and heals. When you choose to live in love, then you will experience the full glory of who you really are and who you can be. You have to be alert to feel the love of everything around you. You have to be aware of everything that's around you. If you are walking down the street listening to the thoughts in your head, you miss it all. This is what is happening to people most of the time. You are either feeling good because you are full of love, or you are feeling bad because you are empty of love. All your feelings are degrees of love. The purpose of your life is to love!

We are ever evolving consciousness which, at its core, in its natural state of being is love, pure love. Earth is ascending, our consciousness is also ascending. We are remembering that we are beings of light and love who are one with everything and god. The most important thing is loving while you are alive. You need to apply love to all areas of your life. Feel love for your life, for the people of the world, and most of all, for yourself. You must learn to love yourself first, before you can love another and love the world.

Love is the greatest power in the universe. Love is also the highest frequency or vibration. The feeling of love is the highest frequency or vibration you can omit. If you could wrap every thought in love, if you could love everything and everyone, your life would be transformed. Love is the power of the world. Every time you give love, you increase and multiply the love in the magnetic field around you. The more you give love and feel good, the more magnetic your field becomes and the more it expands, drawing everything and everyone you love to you. Without exception, every person who has a great life used love to achieve it. Love is the power to have all the positive and good things in life. Love is the greatest power in the universe. Love is not a feeling, love is a positive force. Love is the positive force of life. You are always connected to everything in life through the force of love.

Some people say the law of attraction is really the law of love. The law of attraction or the law of love, they are one and the same. The law of attraction is the law of love. You can get to a point where the magnetic power in your field is so positive and strong that you can have a flash of imagining and feeling something good, and within no time it has appeared in your life, that is the power of love. If you love with all your heart and soul, if you become love itself, then anything is possible for you in this world. Selfless pure love is the only expression of divine perfection we have in this world, it is the greatest power one can possess. The purpose of life is joy, and the greatest joy in life is giving your love. There will be peace and love on earth when there is peace and love in our hearts.

Unconditional love is the love that springs forth when the mind has fallen silent and for once we are free from things like fear and judgment. Unconditional love is always there at our core, it is part of our inner essence. The greatest gift you can give yourself is unconditional love. As you love yourself unconditionally, it will be easier to love others unconditionally.

Dreams

Everyone dreams, even if the dreams are not recalled or remembered when we awaken. If you pay attention to your dreams, your subconscious will reveal in the dream state the issues that you need to resolve in your waking life. From first thing in the morning until last thing at night, the conscious mind registers and responds to the data delivered by our senses of sight, smell, touch, taste, and hearing. In the dream state the subconscious can retrieve and further process this data. By keeping notes about your dreams and reviewing them you should see a pattern emerging that reveals the issues that your subconscious mind perceives as serious. When you start a diary of your dreams, it is also important to keep a diary of some sort of your waking life. If you compare this to your dreams, you should be able to see how the two fit together. Just before you go to sleep say to yourself that you wish to remember clearly any dreams that you have during your sleep. If you keep making this affirmation, you will soon find it easier to remember your dreams. The contents of a dream can vanish in minutes unless you write them down immediately. So if you wake up from a dream during the night, record it at once. When you wake refreshed and clear headed, chances are that during your dream state you have examined an aspect of your life and clarified it. Feeling confused upon waking might be a sign that the issue is still relevant and you are not sure how to deal with it. The subconscious will then continue to use different dreams to give you the opportunity to resolve the matter. Your protective subconscious is trying to help you achieve clarity. Meditation can prepare you for a good nights sleep and for the dream state. There are many breathing techniques to relax you in preparation for either meditation or sleep.

You are able to reprogram your life through your dreams. Tell yourself that you are healthy, abundant, etc. and as you fall asleep, fall asleep with a feeling of abundance, and a feeling of being safe, and a feeling of being nurtured. These feelings will carry on in your dreams and into the next day. Go to sleep with the creation of these feelings and they will manifest. Using dreams, you can create the very next day. You can also do this with day dreams, these are dreams you have while you are awake with your eyes closed and your body in a relaxed position.

When death approaches we may look back upon this life and realize it was just a dream, our entire life was just a kind of dream. Kind of like the dreams we have at night. Then the goal of life would be to wake up from this dream. When we are awakened within the dream, the ego earth drama comes to an end. So we must awaken from the dream. To awaken from within the dream is our purpose now.

Breath

Breath work helps rise awareness, and helps turn your direction away from the material world to the non physical world. Breath is the connection between mind and body.

Breathing Exercise:

This breathing exercise is called "Squeeze out more air". Please do this breathing exercise everyday this week. The secret of increasing breath is to increase exhalation, rather than to extend inhalation. You have greater control over exhalation, and the muscles controlling it are more powerful. By squeezing out more air from your lungs, you will automatically take more air in. Take a deep breath through your nose. Let it out through your month, and when you get to the end, try squeezing a little more air out. Now squeeze out a little more. Now breathe in and let the air expand your lungs normally.

If you practice this exercise regularly, you will deepen and lengthen the period of exhalation until it equals inhalation. Typically, inhalation takes longer than exhalation. In doing so, you will be moving much more air in and out of the lungs, making you breath deeper, slower, and more regular. The more air you move out, the more air you will take in.

This is another breath exercise you can do informally, any time, while waiting in line, sitting at a stoplight, watching TV, or listening to a lecture. It is a good way to take a little break from the normal flow of thoughts, images, and attention to external stimuli, putting your mind briefly in a neutral place. Over time your breath will change in that direction, and you will feel better in both mind and body. Your nervous system will function more smoothly, and your body will operate more harmoniously.

Meditation

In each communing with god you get a little more each time your soul touches the universal soul or god. Outward thinking develops the physical qualities and desires of man, while inward thinking unfolds the spiritual qualities which have been waiting to unfold for the long ages of man's slow journey to the light of his own divinity.

Mindfulness

When you feel fear, put it aside, it means you are living in the past or future, not in the now, not in the present moment. Remember that there is only one important time and that is now. The present moment is the only time over which we have dominion. How can we live in the present moment, meaning live right now. The answer is, we must practice mindfulness. Too much individualism, subjectivity, and attention to one's own self interest creates veils and closes the windows of mindfulness. If you don't want to suffer, if you don't want to be tormented by regret, the only solution is to live every minute you are given in a deep way. That's all there is to it. The only way to deal with insecurity, fear, and suffering is to live in the present moment in a profound way. If you do that, you will have no regrets. Most of us are living like dead people. We move about life in our own corpse because we are not living life in it's entirety. We live a kind of artificial life, with lots of plans, lots of worries and fear. Never are we able to establish ourselves in the here and now and live our lives fully. We have to wake up. We have to make it possible for this moment of awareness to manifest. Make this the most magnificent and wonderful moment of your life. This present moment must become the most wonderful moment in your life. All you need to do is free yourself from the worries and preoccupations about the past and the future.

Meditation Exercise and Mindfulness Exercise:

This week we will be combining the meditation exercise with the mindfulness exercise. Please do this meditation five or ten minutes twice a day for the entire week, in the morning when you first get up and again in the evening. One quickly learns how to select subjects of meditation that fit the situation. Subjects of meditation like love, compassion, emptiness, non attachment, all these belong to the categories of meditation which have power to heal and to reveal. Meditation on these subjects, however can only be successful if we have built up a certain power of concentration, a power achieved by the practice of mindfulness in everyday life. For this meditation I would like you to use the subject of love, just meditate on love, put your focus and attention on love while meditating. Feel the love, be the love, and let yourself be submersed in love.

Feelings and Emotions

Purification means getting rid of the toxins in your life, toxic emotions, toxic thoughts, and toxic relationships. Be able to let go of everything. It's not letting go that is the trap. Every emotion that you feel is about your alignment or misalignment with the energy of your source. Your emotions are your indicators. Pay attention to your emotions. If you are experiencing any lack in your life, look and see if you have a past desire or belief or if you are not happy with the current situations in life. Release this and allow the universe to find you more abundance. Any past pain, hurt, and bad feeling restrict your flows, so you need to remove these to open up you flows.

Feeling and Emotions Exercise:

The practice of letting go. If there are things that are causing you to suffer, you have to know how to let go of them. Happiness can be attained by letting them go. When you have an idea that is making you suffer, you should let go of it, even if it is an idea about your own happiness. You imagine that certain conditions are necessary to your happiness, but deep looking will reveal to you that those notions are the very thing standing in the way of happiness and are making you suffer.

The secret of happiness is being able to let go of your things. You should call your things by their true name. I assure you that when you have let your things go, you will experience happiness, because the more freedom you have, the more happiness you have. The Buddha taught us that joy and pleasure are based on surrender, on letting go. "I am letting go" is a powerful practice. Are you able to let go of things? If not, your suffering will continue.

For this exercise find something in your life that is causing you to suffer and take whatever time you need, but you must let it go, and you must be committed to letting it go. You must have the courage to practice letting go. You must develop a new habit, the habit of realizing freedom. You must identify the things that are causing you to suffer. You must regard them as bonds of slavery. When you have an idea that is making you suffer, you should let go of it. Please do this exercise now and use it in the future when it is needed. If you have several things you would like to let go of, you can do this exercise several times over the next few days.

Mind

When the mind is enlightened, the spirit is free and the body matters not. It's all in our mind. The problem is we think we are our minds. This is not true, we are not our minds. When you recognize that there is a voice in your head that pretends to be you and never stops speaking, you are awakening out of your unconscious identification with the stream of thinking. When you notice that voice, you realize that who you are is not the voice, the thinker, but the me who is aware of it. Since everything in your life is a product of your mind, you can make any desired changes or alterations. You have the power, right now, to effect great miracles in your life and in those around you. The outer mirrors the inner, meaning the outer world is a reflection of the inner world or your inner state of being.

Thoughts

Deliberately guiding your thoughts is the key to a joyful life, but a desire to feel joy is the best plan of all. Because in the reaching for joy, you find the thoughts that attract the wonderful life you desire. When you change your thinking process, everything in your life will also change. You'll be amazed and delighted to see how people, places, things, and circumstances can change. You must have a definite purpose. You must make up your mind as to what you want and where you want to go.

Everything you think about yourself manifests in your reality in this lifetime or the next. Everything you say and everything you do creates who you are. When you think of your friends, think of their good points, not only because that is a much healthier state of mind for you, but because by doing so you strengthen them. When you are reluctantly compelled to recognize the presence of some evil quality in a friend, take special care not to think of it, but think instead of the opposite virtue which you wish them to develop. Avoid negative thoughts and speech about others as the vibration which you will send them will simply make matters worse. Make it a practice to set aside a little time each day devoted to formulating good thoughts about other people, and sending them to these people.

Mind Exercise:

This mind exercise is called "Inspiration". When the mind is well trained and can concentrate on an object, and can maintain its one pointedness for some short time, the next stage is to drop the object, and to maintain the mind in this attitude of fixed attention without the attention being directed to anything. The dropping out of objects of consciousness in the lower worlds is thus followed by the appearance of objects or inspirations of consciousness in the higher worlds. These are the inspirations of genius. So concentrate on an object for a short time and then drop the object and just concentrate. Please try this for five or ten minutes everyday for this entire week.

Energy

Your role is to utilize energy, that is why you exist. You are an energy flowing being, a source or focus, and a receiver. You are a creator. There are just opportunities to focus. You are on the leading edge of thought. Source is flowing through you. You can be joyful in any endeavor where you decide to allow the energy to flow. In men under maya (remember maya means illusion), the flow of life energy is towards the outward world, the currents are wasted and abused in the senses. Man should strive gradually to redirect his energies upward from matter to spirit.

Everything in the universe is made up of energy and this energy vibrates at different frequencies. When you are vibrating in harmony with your souls highest emotions, you embark on an exhilarating ride to all that is good about life. There is a current that's flows and runs through everything. You should use your feelings, this will tell you if you are connected. If you feel good, you are connected. If you feel bad, you are not connected. Feel the connection with everything. Feel the love for everything, allow love to enter you, feel the emotion of love.

You do not have to struggle with life, you merely have to flow with it. Just open your flows, feel your connection and flow with it. Anytime you are feeling good, you are flowing with it, this is like swimming down stream with the current. If you are feeling bad, then you are flowing against it, this is like swimming up stream against the current.

Flows

You are a being composed of light, love, and intelligence. These characteristics are the essence of pure energy. You are an energetic being. Your thoughts control the energy flow within and around you. Whatever you think about determines how you feel and what you experience. To the degree that you feel blessed and expect good things to flow, this is how much and how quickly things will come to you. Let go of any resistance you have to being in and receiving from the stream. The stream is constantly flowing to you, you only have to allow it, feel it, and go with it. Learn to follow the quiet voice within that speaks in feelings rather that words. Follow what you feel or hear inside. Let go of worry, fear, doubt, and disappointment. One needs to flow, to find peace and happiness in life again.

The greater the harmony of life, the greater will be the inflow of that life in each of its parts that are given expression. Then you're tapped into the creative flow of energy in the universe. The real purpose of life is to become spiritually aware and to flow with the currents of life which contribute to the fulfillment of life purposes.

Once again, anytime you are feeling good, you are flowing with it, this is like swimming down stream with the current. If you are feeling bad, then you are flowing against it, this is like swimming up stream against the current.

Energy Exercise:

This energy exercise will involve your feelings, or I should say your state of feeling. We are going to try and feel love and our connection with everything. I would like you to do this for five or ten minutes everyday this week. Sit still, as if you were going to meditate, however this is not a meditation. The feeling of love often comes from the heart area of our body. I want you to use your feelings and see if you can feel love, and feel your connection to everything. Feel love for everything, be at one with everything, and just flow. Try to feel this in your heart. This may take some practice as we are people of the mind and are not use to using our feelings. But try this everyday and after several days you should start to feel this love and connection with everything.

Stress

Stress is fear. Do not be afraid of life. Your inner goal is joy, love, harmony, and peace. Harmony is being at peace with yourself. You are the only power in your world and you can create a peaceful, loving, joyful, and fulfilling life. So train yourself to always think thoughts that make you feel good, that way you will always be creating your life out of joy and in joy. Then you are in the process of making positive changes in all areas of your life. You can and should create a stress free world for yourself.

Stress Exercise:

This is a simple exercise to remove stress. Use this exercise whenever you feel stress in your life. Just sit comfortably and concentrate on your breath. If thoughts come in, bring your awareness back to your breath. Do this for five or ten minutes or until you feel the stress has left you. Please try this exercise now. This is an exercise you should use whenever it is needed in the future to relieve a stressful situation.

Additional Helpful Information – Toxic Relationships

Toxic relationships and toxic environments are those people and places that are harmful to you, meaning people and places that are attempting to cause you harm, upset, or damage you in any manner.

When we are around toxic people or in a toxic environment, we tend to have more accidents as anything toxic is of a lower vibration and will pull you down, lowering your vibrational state. This lowered vibrational state can also lead to sickness and will make you ill. This is your body and being having a negative reaction to the toxic people or toxic places. However, most of the time we do not realize that it was the toxic people or toxic places that made us sick, as the illness may not show up for one, two, three or more days after having the negative lower vibrational exposure. The time delay is why we do not associate the illness with these toxic people or toxic places. Toxic people tend to pull us out of the present moment. Due to this, things like stubbing your toe, banging your finger, walking into something, all the way up to things like a car accidents occur because the person is not in the now, not in the present moment.

Toxic people tend to speak in vague and general terms, they like spreading bad news, they tend to make communications worse, and they often support destructive people and groups. Toxic people often lie, steal things, and will destroy the property of others. These are all very negative and lower vibrational activities. Toxic people can be the person you are having a relationship with, or a family member, or a friend, or someone you work with. I have ended several relationships due to the other person often causing me upset, pain, and problems. If the other person in your relationship is often causing you upset, pain, and problems, it is a toxic relationship. Sadly, it is friends and family members that sometimes cause us the most upset and the most harm in our lives. Friends and family members sometimes do things to us that they would not do to a complete stranger. I have a relative who likes to cause me upset and always justifies their actions with a stupid comment like "Oh well" or "These things happen" or "It is for your own good". How does this person know what is good for me? They seem to think that upsetting my world is for my own good. This same person has never even once apologized for their inconsiderate, mean, or unkind comments or actions, even when I have confronted them and explained how inconsiderate, mean, or unkind they are sometimes. They can not even acknowledge doing any wrong and seem to think that I am being mean to them. This person always has some strange way to justify their actions even when they are clearly in the wrong. It just goes to show how a lower vibrational person thinks, acts, reacts, and what they are capable of.

Toxic people enjoy saying unkind things to others, talking badly of others, hurting others, causing others pain, and damaging things. Toxic people are only happy when they are causing trouble and upsetting others. This makes them feel that they are in power and in control of others, and to some extent this is true. If you confront the toxic person about the situation, they will put the blame on someone else, remember toxic people often lie. When they are causing you trouble and upsetting you, they are stealing your energy and lowering your vibrational level. So they feel better and you feel worse. When these people are trying to make you feel bad, you have to shine brighter, and not allow them to take your energy and lower your vibration. Remember toxic people are in a low vibrational state.

People who have mood swings usually do so because they have had contact with a toxic person even if they don't realize it. They can wake up bright and happy, then run into a toxic person who lowers their vibrational level causing them to become upset and depressed. This lowered state may last for several hours, or a day or two, then the person recovers and is bright and happy again. Several days later they run into the same or another toxic person and once again their vibrational level drops and they are again upset and depressed. This cycle will continue until you realize there is a toxic person causing you to have mood swings. Once you discover who the toxic person is, you can protect yourself by limiting or avoiding contact with this person.

When dealing with toxic people, you have some choices. You can avoid the person and have little contact, or you can use "Keep it sweet and friendly" technique we learned in an earlier chapter, and finally you can sever the connection from the person and never see them again. Sometimes, if it is a family member or a person you work with, it is difficult to sever the connection, as you will have to see this person from time to time. In this case the "Keep it sweet and friendly" technique should help.

I have another relative that I run into sometimes who likes to do things to me that I dislike and that sometimes causes me pain and suffering. This person has done many inconsiderate and thoughtless things to me and other family members. I have mentioned to this person several times that I dislike some of their words and actions, but they do not even comprehend or acknowledge the issue, they just look at me like I am at fault. This person has never once apologized for their actions. This person seems to get a thrill out of upsetting myself and other family members. I have come to realize that this person can not take any responsibility for their actions due to their low vibrational level. So I just had to accept where this person is and realize that since they are a relative and I do have to see them sometimes, that it is best to limit my exposure and conversation with this person. When I do talk to them I use the "Keep it sweet and friendly" technique to save myself from additional unhappiness with this person. This person is trying to pull me down to their level. I have come to realize this and now I just deal with it and do not let them upset me.

If you are a business owner or business manager and you often experience delays, set backs, problems, or other issues at your place of business, look closely at the people involved. You will find that there is one or more toxic people working for you. Toxic people love to delay things, cause set backs, cause problems, and cause other negative issues. Once again, it gives them the sense of being in power and in control. If you confront the toxic person about the situation, they will put the blame on someone else. The best way to handle this situation, is to move the toxic person out of the environment, or better yet, move them out of the company. This will clear up any delays, set backs, problems, or other issues. If you still find there are problems, look and see if there is another toxic person around.

When dealing with toxic places or environments, this could be your home or work, or any place you go to often. You really only have two choices, you can sever the connection and never go to this place again, or you have to learn to deal with the toxic environment. The sever the connection is easy, you just never go there again. Sometimes if your place of work is very toxic, you may have to consider looking for a new and better place to work or you will have to learn to deal with it. Dealing with it means, understanding the place is toxic and not letting it effect you or upset you. I once worked in a toxic environment and had to deal with it for two and one half years, as I had signed a contract for two and one half years. When my contract was up, the employer wanted me to renew for another two and one half years. I said "No" and ran away as fast as I could from that place and have never been back or had any contact with anyone there. I severed the connection permanently of both the toxic place and the toxic people. Often a place is toxic due to it having many toxic people there. Remember toxic people are at a low vibrational level and people tend to be with others who are at a similar vibrational level.

CHAPTER

Cause

The principle of cause and effect states that nothing happens by chance. Everything in the universe has an identifiable cause. When something appears to occur by chance, it means that the cause is unrecognized. Every cause has its effect and every effect has its cause. We can break any chain of cause and effect our own misdeeds have created, if we turn from these misdeeds. Therefore, the same law that closed our prison doors, reversed, can open them.

Yes You Can

We have all grown up in a world where, since we were born, we have been told things and heard things like "No", "Don't do that", "Don't try that", "Don't touch that", "You can't do that", "Do what I say", etc. Another words, we have been programmed for failure and limitation since we were born. No one ever said things like "Yes", "Do that", "Try that", "Touch that", "Do what you feel is right", "You can do it". Our parents and the other people we have known in our lives are not even aware that they have been filling us with negative programming. It's what their parents did to them, and what their parents parents did to them, etc. This is the way most of us have been raised throughout time. It's no wonder that we are afraid to try things, because we have been programmed to be afraid, we have been programmed for failure and limitation. I am here to tell you that "Yes you can", "Yes, you can do it", you can change the negative programming to positive programming.

Caution can be another problem. Of course using caution when it is appropriate makes a lot of sense. You would not cross the street without looking both ways to ensure no cars were coming. To not do so would be foolish, as you could get run over. However, too much caution is really fear, it will hinder you and prevent you from doing things. That's like saying "No, I'm not going to do something because I may fail". If you try doing the thing, you may fail, but you may also succeed, the choice is yours. If you don't even try doing the thing in the first place, you have already failed by default.

Choices

Choice means giving up something you want for something you want more. Life is full of choices. You are being presented with the very situations around you, as well as the precise issues inside you, that must be resolved in order for your new reality to be completely realized. Your beliefs influence the choices you make. Your beliefs set into motion inner processes and behaviors that influence how you move, act, and feel. What you believe, you receive. You must overcome negative beliefs that hold you back. Every person and all the events of your life are there because you have drawn them to you. What you choose to do with them is up to you. The actions you take will shape your future for better or worse. Such is the power of choice for we all have free will. If you choose to do something that is good, it will make your life better. If you choose to do something that is bad, it will make your life worst. Any condition can be changed for the better. If you believe that something is good and you do it, it benefits you. Get clear and happy about whatever choice you make and it will be yours. They say the choices we make define us. You make your choices and you live with them, and in the end you are your choices. Remember, there is no fate, but what we make for ourselves.

Impossible and difficult situations in our lives are often created because we are off purpose. Many people have no idea what their true purpose is. The truth is that purpose becomes clear when we are ready to live our lives creatively and fully express our greater self. Each one of us has a purpose, a chosen life from the moment we are born. In order to discover our purpose or creative intention, we must believe and trust that a creative intelligence is seeking to create through us. You must have a definite purpose. You must make up your mind as to what you want and where you want to go. All we have to do is decide what to do with the time that is given us. You are either living or dying, living is doing whatever you want to do, dying is everything else. Mark Twain said "The two most important days of your life are the day you were born and the day you find out why".

Desire

Want or desire is to focus attention or give thought towards a subject while at the same time experiencing positive emotion. When you give your attention to something and feel only positive emotion about it, it will come very quickly into your experience. The thoughts that you think in combination with the feelings of strong emotion are the most powerful. Give forth thought with positive emotion and you become the most powerful of all magnets.

When you hold the desire to be joyful and are sensitive to the way you feel, and guide your thoughts in the direction of things that feel better and better, you improve your vibration, thus your point of attraction becomes stronger and you attract the things you desire. Deliberately guiding your thoughts and feelings is the key to a joyful life, but a desire to feel joy is the best plan of all. Because in the reaching for joy, you find the thoughts and feelings that attract the wonderful life you desire. Become a being who thinks only of that which he is wanting, who speaks only that which he is wanting, who does only that which he is wanting, and therefore brings forth only joyful emotions. Words alone do not attract, but when you feel strong positive emotion about the words you speak, your vibration will grow stronger and the law of attraction must answer those vibrations.

By deliberately directing your thoughts and feelings, rather than merely observing what is happening around you, you will begin to change the vibrational patterns to which the law of attraction is responding. Thus you will become a powerful creator of your own experience and you will experience substantial change in your life. There is nothing you can not be, do, or have.

Inspired

Divine inspiration is the birth right of every human being. We are all very special, we just do not know or remember this. We must change our beliefs. When an idea occurs to you and you feel eagerness about it, that means that your inner being is a vibrational match to the idea. Your positive emotion is what inspiration is. Pure desire is always accompanied by positive emotion. There were times in your life when you felt inspired. You felt like you were doing something worth while. Do things that inspire you. You should be able to feel inspired with everything that you do. And when you feel inspired while you are doing something there is no way you can not succeed. The key is inspiration, so feel inspired always.

Inspired Action

When you get an inspired feeling to take action, you need to take action and not wait, act right now. Action is fun. There is no action in all of the universe more delicious than inspired action. The secret of enjoying life is to take an interest in it. Now for anything to interest us we must enter into the spirit of it. One of the things that happens as we grow older is we lose our spirit of play, our sense of play, our sense of having fun. We must recapture this spirit of play for it keeps us young. When you have the spirit of play, you feel alive, and everything and everyone around you senses this in you. The world is at your call and will do whatever you desire. Children have this, but we lose it as we grow older. Rediscover this spirit of play. To enjoy anything we must enter into the spirit of it. To enjoy the living quality of life, we must enter into the spirit of life itself. When we awaken to the fact that our true place in the universe is to be fellow creators with god in carrying on the work of creation, then we see that up to this time we have entirely missed the purpose of our calling.

Imagination

To create a better world, we must start with ourselves. We are the imagination of ourselves. Visualization is very important in altering and reshaping one's destiny. We are constantly creating when we use our imagination, but when this activity is not appropriately selective, we may tend to limit our possibilities by capturing images from our past and creating the same situations in the future. It is the fears of tomorrow and the regrets of yesterday that rob us of today. We must avoid dictating and creating our future out of our past. This world is but a canvas to our imagination.

The degree to which we assume something is possible or impossible is largely controlled by our imagination. Only we can govern whether our selective imagining is positive or negative. When using the imagination negatively by reliving the pains of the past (fears, guilt, and feelings of anger or unworthiness), we automatically limit our circle of possibility. The subconscious proceeds to keep us in a prison of negativity by implementing similar experiences to coincide with this understanding of reality. In essence, we create an unhappy insecure present by picturing past sadness and perceived failure, and then we try to form our future from a present state of mind that is build upon those negative images of the past.

Only our imagination limits its potential. You can choose how you are going to use your imagination. You can remember whatever parts of the past you want, and play in advance the future you desire.

By selectively applying your imagination, you can focus on positive experiences from the past and use these images to form a solid base for the future. Perceiving a positive future not only shows us how to get where we want to go but actually draws us towards the people, circumstances, places, and conditions to fulfill our image of the future. We must actively imagine the future we desire with ourselves as the key players. Visualize the future you want for yourself and charge it with the energy of concentration. Proper visualization with the use of concentration and will power enables us to materialize thoughts, not only as dreams or visions in the mental realm, but also as experiences in the material realm. Before you can change a situation, we must first change our perception. Changing our perception requires being open to expansion. We must open the channels of creativity fully. All of us have creative and intuitive abilities and moments of inspiration. When these moments are upon us, attempt to look within and feel the flow of mental energies passing through your mental space. When we are focused on what we really want, our vision becomes clear and clarity is the point of power.

Visualization

When you focus your mind on the result you want, your brain will facilitate desirable directions and opportunities that will ultimately get you where you want to go. Visualization has a more profound impact on your subconscious mind than you might realize. Your subconscious mind does not distinguish between whether you are imagining something or actually experiencing it. You can make changes in your opinions, beliefs, and levels of expectation by vividly imagining the experiences and circumstances you select. We move towards what we picture in our mind and the intention drives us as an energy source. Where ever the mind goes the energy flows. Whatever you give your energy to is what you will have more of. We don't get what we want, we get what we expect. Forget your worries, forget your fears, in place of them, visualize the conditions you would like to see. Realize their availability, declare to yourself that you already have all these things that you desire, that your needs have been met. Believe that ye receive it, and ye shall have it. When we play in advance in our minds what we expect with positive feelings, our subconscious is compelled to find a way to make it possible.

Active visualization, with yourself as an active participant, is a key step in the process of transitioning from a sense of lack to a sense of abundance. Visualization can make your life sensational. When we envision ourselves having what we want, we play it in advance in our minds as truly possible. Change your inner self and you change the outer or your life. The reality you now experience is the result of what you think of yourself. We create our own reality and physical experience. You can sit quietly and visualize whatever you want to create for yourself. See it happening to you now in that moment. Thought creates exactly what you think, so if you visualize something happening in the future, it will always be happening in the future and never in the now. You must create in the now. You must believe you have it now. Remember, you must have positive feelings and emotions for whatever you are visualizing.

Breath

While you are sleeping, accumulations of suffering will reveal themselves to you in your dreams. Depression, fear, and confusion may also manifest in the body. You will have headaches and all kinds of other aches and pains. Buddhism teaches that the body and mind are two aspects of the same thing. The cells of your body are not only physical, they are also mental, they are both at the same time. Feel the breath as energy.

Breathing Exercise:

This breathing exercise is called "Energy breath". Its purpose is to raise the energy of the nervous system and increase alertness. The idea is to breathe in and out rapidly, through the nose, keeping your mouth lightly closed. Inhalation and exhalation should be of equal length, and as short as possible. Get in as many as two or three breathes per second if you can do that comfortably. You will find that this is real exercise, the muscles may become tired, and your body temperature may increase. At first, do not do the energy breath for any longer than ten seconds. After that breathe normally for awhile. Each time you do it, you can increase the time by about five seconds, until you have worked up to thirty seconds. Try it now for ten seconds and see how your mind and body feel. Use this whenever you wish to increase your energy and alertness.

Meditation

Anyone who decides to lead a spiritual life must daily devote some time to meditation. Only to the mind concentrated and shut out from the world, can the divine reveal itself. Allow your attention to return to the breathing when it wanders during meditation. We use the breath as a way to still ourselves and become peaceful. Meditation is the simple process of quietly looking within. Most of the time our attention is turned outward. We engage the world we see through our physical senses. But if we wish to understand our minds, we must occasionally look within. In meditation the attention is withdrawn from the sight, sounds, and other stimuli coming from the external world.

Meditation Exercise:

For this meditation we will be using the spiritual eye often called the third eye. If you close your eyes, take a few deep breaths, and place your attention on the area between your two physical eyebrows, you will begin to see or feel an oval shaped object lying on its side, this is your spiritual eye or third eye. Please try this now.

Do this meditation twice a day for the entire week, in the morning when you first get up and again in the evening. This is a Mantra meditation using the Sanskrit mantra "Hong Sau". With your eyes closed, look into the spiritual eye or third eye center, by concentrating at the spiritual eye center between the eyebrows. Then begin with "Hong", let the first word float in your awareness when you breathe in. Let the second word "Sau" float in your awareness when you breathe out. Listen to the mantra until awareness of it ceases or you go beyond it into deep silence. See instructions below.

When awareness is partially or completely removed from identification with mental processes, superconsciousness is experienced. Superconsciousness is a natural state to the soul. The reason many souls do not know this, is because their attention is identified with mental processes to the extent that they have forgotten their real inner nature. Meditation is helpful because it helps us reconnect with our superconsciousness. Repeated superconscious occurrences eventually purify our mental field, resulting in mental illumination and the removal of all delusions and illusions. Use of meditation techniques such as prayer, mantra, contemplation of inner light and or sound will enable you to remove attention from outer sources of distraction and bring you to a place where spontaneous meditation can occur.

Meditation should be practiced daily. The easiest way to ensure regularity of practice is to meditate early in the morning, before thinking about the day's duties and projects. Ten to fifteen minute sessions will clear awareness, calm mental processes, reduce stress, calm the nervous system, strengthen the immune system, and enliven the systems of the body. When meditating for the purpose of experiencing refined conscious states, sit for a longer time. After practicing a meditation technique, rest in the tranquil silence for awhile.

The easiest way to meditate is to listen to a mantra, a pleasant word or word phrase that will attract your attention and keep it focused. Sit comfortably, poised and upright, with your spine straight. Inhale more deeply than usual, then exhale. Do this two or three times. Relax and be still. With your eyes closed, look into the spiritual eye or third eye center, by concentrating at the spiritual eye center between the eyebrows. Be aware of your natural breathing rhythm. Mentally recite the mantra with inhalation and exhalation. When using a word phrase mantra, mentally recite or listen to the first word "Hong" with inhalation and to the second word "Sau" with exhalation. As your body becomes relaxed, and thoughts and emotions are quieted, breathing will be slower and thoughts and emotions will be less distracting. If your attention wanders, bring it back to the mantra. When your mind is quiet, disregard the mantra and rest in the peaceful silence for the duration of the meditation session. If thoughts, moods, or random mental images interfere with concentration, or if you become too passive and only semiconscious, resume the use of the mantra until you are again alert and meditation flows smoothly.

The purpose of meditation is to calm subconscious impulses which cause thoughts and emotions to occur. When awareness is clear and concentration is steady, superconsciousness devoid of thoughts and emotions will be experienced. When using a word phrase mantra, mentally recite or listen to the first word with inhalation and to the second word with exhalation. Remember to allow inhalation and exhalation to occur naturally. The Sanskrit mantra "Hong Sau" is easy to use and it's vibratory potency has a calming effect on the mind. Use the same mantra each time you meditate. Devotional prayer, breath awareness, and listening to a mantra, are all helpful to quiet the mind.

Feelings and Emotions

Every thought, emotion, and desire vibrates and attracts experiences of matching vibration. If you'd like to attract better experiences, you must elevate your thoughts and emotions thus raising your vibration. When an idea occurs to you and you feel eagerness about it, that means that your inner being is a vibrational match to the idea. Your positive emotion is what inspiration is. When you give your attention to something and feel only positive emotion about it, it will come very quickly into your experience. Pure desire is always accompanied by positive emotion. Each thought, emotion, or mental state vibrates at different frequencies, so you can choose to deliberately hold specifically high vibrating thoughts, emotions, and mental states. Similarly you can raise the vibrations of objects and thoughts to move them to higher planes of existence.

Feeling and Emotions Exercise:

This is an imagination and visualization exercise. Please try this for five or ten minutes everyday this week. Imagination and visualization can be used to change negative feelings. Are you sad? Try closing your eyes and thinking about images that you associate with happy times. As these images appear, they will evoke the emotional energy patterns you felt during those happier times. You will be creatively pulling positive emotional energies into your conscious mind where they will replace the negative ones that have their hold on you. Imagination and visualization can also be used to bring about changes in your life. Imagine yourself as you want to be. By this process you will establish new energy patterns within your own mind. In time these new patterns will actually begin to affect the way you operate in your life. Using the imagination, you can literally change your own psychological make up so that you become more the person that you want to be. The energies that form mental patterns have effects beyond the physical and mental realms. Your thoughts play an important part in determining which events and situations manifest in your life. So, lets use this exercise to replace any negative feelings you have with positive feelings.

You can use imagination to enter more deeply into non physical realms. For example, you can initiate out of body experiences with the imagination. If you close your eyes and vividly imagine that you are somewhere else, you begin to transfer your conscious focus from your physical body to your traveling body.

Mind

It appears that the mind is the real problem, that's what keeps us down and suppressed. That's what keeps us from enlightenment. The mind should be a tool, but it has gone out of control, thinking it is in charge of the person, creating all kinds of mental noise and making us feels bad. Whatever thoughts come into your head are not really important, its just mental noise most of the time. The mind is like a radio that plays constantly, tuning itself from one station to the next. Taming our mind doesn't necessarily mean turning off the mind noise. Rather it entails recognizing the noise as separate from us, so that when it plays something we do not like, we have the power to change the channel and choose what we want to listen to. The mind is very active, it goes on and on, it never stops. This is mind noise or mental noise.

Most of the noise is not necessary. You have a noise machine in your head. Most of these thoughts are in regards to problems, but may not be current problems, and this is normal to most people.

When you can't stop thinking of the problem, or when troubling thoughts and memories arise without your intent, it's not your brain working, but your mind wandering. Then the mind controls you and it will run wild. Realize this is man's prison, he is not in control of his thoughts or his life. This is mental noise and it is usually negative. Your mind, not other people or your surroundings, is the source of your moods and troubles. If you remain blind to this weaknesses, the noise will go on forever. Your slave like obedience to the mind's moods and impulses is a serious error.

Many people do not understand how thought and health are linked. All illness and all wellness are equally the result of the way we think. Thoughts and feelings affect our emotional bodies and create vibrations of harmony or disharmony. This in turn affects the physical body. When we keep our thoughts constructive, kind, and loving, we are happy. Happiness brings harmony, and living in harmony creates health. Disease is the result of living in disharmony. Anger, anxiety, frustration, disappointment, worry, and stress create thought forms that break down the physical body and make us sick. Many times, illnesses like the common cold and flu are brought upon us because our immune system is weakened as a result of emotional stress. The root cause of our emotional stress can be found in our thinking. When a thought is held for a prolonged period it will manifest. Any thought or emotion held and repeated will bring an equal result. Anger, hatred, bitterness, resentment, envy, and jealousy create powerful thought forms and always result in either a physical or mental disease or disorder. The solution is to turn off the mind. But how do we turn off the mind. When the mind chatters, do not allow it to continue, just stop it. When an evil thought enters the mind, do not fight it, as the mind can think of only one thing at a time, let the mind be turned to a good thought, and the evil thought will be expelled. Chinese philosophy links depression with thinking too much, so give yourself a break.

Thoughts

It has been said that people age more by worry than by work. What is "worry"? It is the process of repeating the same train of thought over and over again with small alterations, coming to no result. It is the continued reproduction of thought forms, initiated by the mind, and imposed on the consciousness. The thinker has dwelt on a painful subject. Replace the worry thought with a positive thought. Monitor your thoughts, if any negative thoughts enter your mind, change them at once to positive thoughts. You can train yourself to do this. When you give thoughts of hate, then others will give that back to you. When you give thoughts of love, others will give that back to you. Every thought you think counts, and everything you say counts. So watch carefully your thoughts and your speech.

The first level of creation is your thoughts. What you think produces energy in the universe, and if you think it often enough and long enough, it will actually produce a physical result in your life. The second level of creation is words. As you speak, so will it be done. Your words are really a form of energy. If you say something often enough, loudly enough, it will come to pass. Our actions are the third level of creation, that which we do. Speech is the process of putting thoughts into forms with language, sound, vibration, and energy. Speech is a major device for bringing things into our lives. Speech should be an exact reflection of our thoughts. Conflict arises when we think one thing and say another. You should watch what you say, and only say things that you wish to happen in your life. Positive thoughts and speech will bring good things into your life and of course negative thoughts and speech will bring bad things into your life. Most people think one thing, say a second thing, and do a third. They do not have it all together. You should monitor your thoughts, words, and actions. You need to learn how to completely control your thinking and your speaking. You need to keep your thinking and your speaking very positive, do not allow anything negative to come in.

Life begins to change for you when you begin to say what you're thinking and do what you're saying. And then you have it all together and you start to create from all three centers of creation. Suddenly you begin to manifest and produce extraordinary results in your life in a very short period of time. Become a being who thinks only of that which he is wanting, who speaks only that which he is wanting, who does only that which he is wanting, and therefore brings forth only joyful emotions and joyful situations in his life.

Mind Exercise:

This is an exercise to handle bad thoughts. If a particular kind of undesirable thought persistently imposes itself on you, then it is wise to provide a special weapon, some verse or phrase that embodies the opposite idea should be chosen, and whenever the objectionable thought presents itself, the phrase should be repeated and dwelt upon. In a week or two the thought will cease to trouble you. Please try this exercise now. Find some bad thought that has been on your mind and use this technique on it. This is an exercise you should use whenever it is needed in the future.

Mindfulness

The highest purpose of the human body is to become a clear channel for the light so that it's brightness can dissolve all obstructions, and all restrictions. Awareness is how the human being experiences the light of consciousness. To expand awareness, to direct attention, to surrender to the light of consciousness, open yourself up to the light of awareness. Practice discipline, do not give into urges. Meditate your actions. Meditating an action is different from doing it. To do, there is a doer, a self conscious someone performing. But when you meditate an action, you've already released attachment to outcomes. There's no you left to do it. In forgetting yourself, you become what you do, so your action is free, spontaneous, without ambition, inhibition, or fear.

Mindfulness Exercise:

This exercise is called an hour of mindfulness. Please do this exercise everyday this week. Set aside one hour a day to practice mindfulness. Do only simple work like house cleaning, garden work, washing clothes, washing your car, etc. Every movement during this time should be at least two times slower than usual. The point is to do one thing at a time two times slower than usual, keeping all of your attention on the one thing that you are doing and do nothing else. Also keep your mind on what you are doing and on nothing else. Then move on to the next activity. If you are washing your car, put all your attention on washing the car. If your mind wanders, bring your attention back to the current activity. Once again, every movement during this time should be at least two times slower than usual. Do this for a full hour each day of the week. After wards sit in meditation for a few minutes before returning to your normal activities. This exercise will help you pull your attention out of the past and the future, keeping you in the present. Think of this as taking a vacation from yourself. You might like the change well enough to make it permanent. If an hour is hard to do, you can start with thirty minutes and work up to an hour.

White Light

We can use white light to protect us from negative vibrations and energy. White light is known esoterically as the highest form of spiritual protection. Since white light is made up of all of the colors of the spectrum, we can say that the consciousness of your being, can be referred to as white light. In other words, the deepest part of who you are is the source of white light, although some people choose to experience it as coming from above. One of the most important aspects of spiritual protection is white light protection. It's very effective at removing and preventing negative energy from harming you. To do this, just visualize an egg-shaped sphere of brilliant white light completely surrounding you, from head to toe. Really focus on seeing it clearly in your mind, and keep building it up so it's super bright and glowing. See it as a solid barrier of protection that negativity cannot cross.

Holistic healers refer to white light as part of the universe that stores all positive energy. By calling on the white light, it is believed that the human energy field can be cleansed and protected from negative energy. Negativity in any form can be damaging to the human energy field. The human energy field is often called the aura. The aura is an electromagnetic field that surrounds every creature that exists, we can call it the human energy field or the aura. Fear, anger, depression, arguments, negative people and places, actually create negative energy that can cling to you or build up in your home and cause problems over time. Spiritual cleansing is very important, for yourself and your home. I recommend they be done at least every few weeks, more if you find yourself feeling stressed or fatigued. Spiritual Protection is something that everyone should know how to do.

White Light Protection Exercise:

Do this white light protection exercise for several minutes everyday this week or whenever you feel you need protection in the future. Some people will do this everyday to protect themselves. Do this exercise now. Surround yourself with love and white light to keep all negative things from touching and affecting you. To do this, just visualize an egg-shaped sphere of brilliant white light completely surrounding you, from head to toe. Really focus on seeing it clearly in your mind, and keep building it up so it's super bright and glowing. See it as a solid barrier of protection that negativity cannot cross. You can do the same for your home or car. I always use this for my home and car. It works on anything.

Additional Helpful Information – Emotional States

A persons emotional state is determined by the predominant emotions that they display during the average day. People who display emotions like enthusiasm, cheerfulness, and love are operating at a higher vibrational level. While people who display emotions like anger, hate, and resentment are operating at a lower vibrational level. Be cautious, a smiling person is not always an indication of a high vibrational level. I have had people smile to my face and then do some awful things. I was going through a difficult situation and I mentioned it to someone I know. This person was thrilled at the fact that I was going through a difficult situation and was suffering. Every time I saw them over the next two weeks they would be smiling from ear to ear, and every twenty minutes they would bring the situation up in conversation. They were trying to keep my mind engaged in the difficult situation, they were enjoying keeping me in a state of pain, and were attempting to lower my vibrational level. Finally after two weeks I had to tell this person that I no longer wanted to talk about this situation. So watch out for the smiling person.

It is better to judge a person based on their emotional state, the things they say, and their behavior, the things they do, and the actions they undertake. People at a high vibrational level are happy when others are doing well, while people at a low vibrational level are happy when others are not doing well, or are suffering, or are in pain. A persons actions is another good way to tell a person vibrational level. People who help others, people who support constructive groups, people who do things to improve the world or parts of it, and people who like to make others happy, bring joy to others, are people of high vibrational levels. People at a high vibrational level are honest and truthful. People who do harm to others, people who often lie, people who steal things, people who like to destroy the property of others, and people who support destructive groups, are people of lower vibrational levels. People at a low vibrational level are dishonest and often lie, they will often do things and then deny doing them, or say that someone else did it. A low vibrational person will not take responsibility for their action, while a high vibrational person will. A low vibrational person almost never says they are sorry, in fact the word sorry is not even in their vocabulary. A person at a low vibrational level usually has no consideration for others, they will make a mess or leave a mess behind them, and never pick things up or clean up after themselves. People at a low vibrational level will often do unkind or harmful things to you and other people, and believe that what they have done is acceptable. However, if you were to do the exact same thing back to them, they would become very upset and act as if you were causing them great harm and pain. People at a low vibrational level will often harm people and animals for no reason. Low vibrational people are usually very sensitive, but not in a good way. If you say something to them, like confront them about a lie they just said, they will become very upset and very defensive, even when they know that you know they are not telling the truth. Low vibrational people also get upset if you try to give them advice or let them know that they are behaving badly, this is due to where they are vibrationally, they think they are always correct and that others are in the wrong. It is very difficult to help someone at a low vibrational level as they think there is nothing wrong with them and that they can do no wrong.

What a person says is also another good indication of their vibrational level. People who have nice things to say to others and about others, people who spread good news, and people who make communications better, are people of a higher vibrational level. People who have bad and unkind things to say to others or about others, people who talk negatively behind the backs of others, people who tend to speak in very broad general terms, people who like spreading bad news, and people who like to worsen communications, are people of a lower vibrational level.

Someone at a low vibrational level may lie and steal. Someone at a very low vibrational level may commit murder. The lower a persons vibrational level, the worst the crime they will commit on other people. All of the criminals, murderers, drug dealers, and people who perform activities like scams and frauds are people at very low vibrational levels, and these are the people you want to avoid. Low vibrational people who behave badly, usually don't even realize they are behaving badly, to them it is just normal behavior. People who are at a very low vibrational level may have hygiene issues, meaning they do not bathe and have very poor cleanliness habits. It is good to have some knowledge of the vibrational level of the people you see and deal with on a daily basis. This will help you understand them and give you an understanding of what to expect from these people. This is also very helpful when selecting a mate like a girlfriend or boyfriend, or when selecting friends, or when selecting business partners. Would you want to marry a person of a low vibrational level knowing that they will bring you down and most likely make your life very difficult. Very often we select our mates and lovers based on their physical appearance, their good looks, or their great body, or for sexual reasons, and not on their vibrational or emotional level. It is best to select mates, lovers, friends, and business partners of a higher vibrational level. This will make your life much more enjoyable and make you a happier person.

CHAPTER

Create

Why are we here? We are here to be creators. We are here to infiltrate space with ideas and creations of thought. We are here to make something of this life. Life isn't happening to you, life is responding to you. Most of us have created a fear based reality, so we do not get what we want. We should be creating our reality based on love. You are the creator of your life. You are the writer of your life story. Whatever we give our attention to, we create more of. By giving attention to your spiritual self, you will expand the capacities of your own created self. This will allow you to handle with confidence and power, any and all impossible situations you may encounter. We have successes and failures, and hopefully we learn from all of them. Through all of it we are guided and taught by the overall spiritual aspect of ourselves, the self, which is who and what we are beyond the limitations of our physical focus. We can change the course of our experiences by changing our mental patterns through conscious effort.

We are still experimenting and playing with our powers of creativity. This world, with its linear time, is a school, where our creations develop slowly so that we can see what we are doing and evolve into the wisdom of the self. The forces we generate are spread out and slowed down so that we can witness the effects of our creative intentions. Time allows us to make adjustments and corrections. We are creators with god and that which we create is an expression of the level of understanding at which we have arrived. What we see is an extension of who and what we are. We are learning to be conscious creators, and the physical dimension is our laboratory. Our experiences of reality mirror our inner states, so that we may see clearly what we are doing and make necessary changes. We reap what we sow, and until we understand that we sow with our minds, we will be kept in the class room of physical reality. You are creating the things in your life. If you do not like the things in your life, just create better things.

If you want to create the life of your dreams, it begins by writing your dreams down and getting as clear as possible about them. If you are not manifesting what you want, change your thoughts and change your feelings. Deliberate creation is about deliberately guiding your thoughts in good feeling directions. The more you maintain these good feeling thoughts, the higher your vibration, the more the law of attraction will deliver to you the things you desire. This will also put you in a position to receive even clearer guidance from your inner source. The more you practice this, the less resistance you will have, and the better your life will be.

Here is the key to creation. See yourself as a magnet, attracting unto you the way you feel at any point in time. When you feel happy you attract happiness. When you feel healthy you attract health. When you feel prosperous you attract prosperity. When you feel loved you attract love. The way you feel is the point of attraction. The best way to predict our future is to create it. The end result is that we always attract what we feel worthy of. When a high state of beingness is turned into a high state of doing in the physical world, one has achieved right livelihood.

Creating Your Day

No master worth their salt ever let the day happen to them, rather, they create their day. If you create your day in advance, with practice, this is how your day will work out. Are you taking the time to create your day? Before you get up in the morning and remember who you are, create your day. Then after you create your day, your routine will change. Just wake up in the morning and consciously create your day the way you want it to happen. This world is but a canvas for our imagination. Creation is only the projection into form of that which already exists. Use your imagination and live as though you already have what you want. This world is your imagination. Where your thinking is, there is your experience. We are constantly in the act of creating who we are. You are in every moment deciding who and what you are. As a man thinks, so is he. When you think badly, the following becomes true, that which I feared is come upon me.

Look well to this day:

> Yesterday is but a dream and tomorrow is only a vision,
> but today well lived makes every yesterday a dream of happiness
> and every tomorrow a vision of hope,
> therefore look well to this day.

So the plan is to make the most of your days and of your time. You can cry about your past mistakes or you can live well this day, and create the future you desire.

Law of Creation

We have the ability to create physical reality out of thin air. In the physical world you can not have a physical experience until you have created it first in thought. Negative emotion exists only when you are miss creating. When this happens stop doing whatever you are doing and focus your thoughts on something that feels better, something positive. We tend to avoid creating miracles by living life through our fears. As you create your new reality, doubts and fears will present themselves. Doubts and fears undermine our commitment to creation. We find ourselves swallowed by anger, envy, and grief over what is not, instead of committing to create what we can be. Doubt and fear allows us to hold on to what we have and convinces us that reaching for our dreams is unsafe. As a result, we remain frozen in the familiar. Anything that you do not want to continue in your life, you must take your attention away from. Clear out all the trash in your mind that can interfere with your creative focus. Do the same for physical things. Clear out those things that can interfere with your creative focus.

See yourself as a magnet, attracting unto you the way you feel. If you feel clear and in control you will attract clarity, if you feel happy you will attract happiness, if you feel healthy you will attract health, if you feel prosperous you will attract prosperity, if you feel love you will attract love. If you want many things at the same time it adds confusion, so focus upon the most important thing you want and the specifying of what you want. The key to success is to have dominant thought patterns that are totally aligned with what you want. This is our creative intention. We move towards what we picture in our mind and the intention drives us as an energy source. Where ever the mind goes the energy flows. Whatever you give your energy to is what you will have more of. Perceiving a positive future not only shows us how to get where we want to go but actually draws us towards the people, circumstances, places, and conditions to fulfill out image of the future.

The first level of creation is your thoughts. What you think produces energy in the universe, and if you think it often enough and long enough, it will actually produce a physical result in your life. The second level of creation is words. As you speak, so shall it be done. Your words are really a form of energy. If you say something often enough, loudly enough, it will come to pass. Our actions are the third level of creation, that which we do. Most people think one thing, say a second thing, and do a third. They do not have it all together and this leads to confusion, therefore they do not get what they want. As we're thinking and speaking, we're creating. You should monitor your thoughts, words, and actions. Get your thoughts, words, and actions off of what is and put them purely on what you want. The more you think and speak and do what you want, the faster what you want will be yours. Life begins to change for you when you begin to say what you're thinking and do what you're saying. Then you have it all together and you start to create from all three centers of creation. Suddenly you begin to manifest and produce extraordinary results in your life in a very short period of time.

As you are moving through your daily experience, set forth the intention to notice things that you like. This turns your thoughts into positive thoughts, helping the creation process. Thoughts that you feel strong emotion about will manifest more quickly in the physical universe. Be sensitive to the way you are feeling. If you want many things at the same time it adds confusion, so focus upon the most important thing you want and the specifying of what you want. As you are moving through a day of intending, you will feel the power and the momentum of your intentions building, and you will find yourself feeling gloriously invincible. As you are seeing yourself in creative control of your own life experience, you will feel as if there is nothing you can not be, do, or have. What this really means, before you do anything, take a moment to see yourself doing what you want, and doing it to the perfect outcome that you want,

Example:

You have to go food shopping, see yourself finding a good parking space, see yourself moving through the store quickly, finding everything that you want, and when you get to the checkout there is no line.

Do this for everything, every action in your life, kind of like planning your next move in advance and predetermining the outcome. When you really want something it comes fast, when you really do not want something it comes even faster. The idea of intending is to set your thought of what you want, focusing upon it clearly enough, in the moment, that you bring forth positive emotions about it. Your clarity brings the speed. You want to ponder your desire so specifically that you bring forth the power of the universe to speed your creation.

As you become more efficient at intending, you will have more hours in your day to do those things you want to do.

The correction which our mode of thinking needs therefore is to start with being, not with having, and we may then trust the having to come along in its right order. Thus our life will become one endless progress, ever widening as we go on. This is the law of expansion. See yourself as the source, rather than the recipient of what it is you would choose to experience in life. When you imagine yourself to be the source of that which you wish to receive you become very resourceful and then you do become a magician. If you want more magic in your life, bring more magic into the room with you. If you want more love in your life, bring more love into the room with you. Be the source, in the lives of others, of that which you would have in your own life.

Stillness

Stillness means no thought, being without thought. Thought is noise, we must turn off the noise. Allow the now to be, accept the now, accept where you are right now. Accept what is and accept it in the now. Surrender to the now, stop thinking, or at least stop paying attention to your thoughts. When you are doing something, your thoughts should be focused on what you are doing and nothing else. When you are doing nothing, your thoughts should be empty, the essence of self. When the mind is devoid of all content, we not only find absolute serenity and peace, we also discover the true nature of the self. The state of absolute emptiness. There is no time, no space, no becoming, just nothingness. Pure experience is the mind seeing itself. This is possible only when the mind is emptiness itself. That is when the mind is devoid of all its possible contents except itself. As I mentioned earlier, how can we know if we are making progress on the spiritual path. The degree of absence of thought is your measure of progress on your spiritual path. That doesn't give you much to think about (that's a joke).

The problems with humans is we identify with our mind. The mind is very active, it goes on and on, it never stops. This is mind noise and most of the noise is not necessary. You have a noise machine in your head. Most of these thoughts are in regards to problems, but they may not be current problems, and this is normal for most people. The problem is we think we are our minds. This is not true, we are not our minds. Life is not suffering, it's just that you will suffer, rather than enjoy it, until you learn to let go of your mind's attachments and just go along for the ride.

When you can't stop thinking of problems, or when troubling thoughts and memories arise without your intent, it's not your brain working, but your mind wandering. Then the mind controls you and it will run wild. Realize this is man's prison, he is not in control of his thoughts or his life. This is mental noise and it is usually negative. Your mind, not other people or your surroundings, is the source of your moods and troubles. If you remain blind to your weaknesses, how can you correct them. Your slave like obedience to the mind's moods and impulses is a serious error. So what are the positive uses of the mind, there aren't any. It appears that the mind is the real problem, that's what keeps us down and suppressed. That's what keeps us from enlightenment. The mind should be a tool, but it has gone out of control, thinking it is in charge of the person, creating all kinds of mental noise, making us feel bad. Learn how to silence the endless chatter of words and thoughts that flow unceasingly through the normal human mind. The solution is to turn off the mind. But how do we turn off the mind. When the mind chatters, do not allow it to continue, just stop it. When the mind becomes filled with thoughts, do not pay attention to them, do not listen to them.

When the mind is silent, and the thoughts, feelings, perceptions, and memories with which we habitually identify have fallen away, then what remains is the essence of self, the pure subject without an object, what we then find is not a sense of "I am this" or "I am that", but just "I am", or pure beingness. In this state you know the essence of self, and you know that essence to be pure consciousness. You know this to be what you really are. You are not a being who is conscious, you are consciousness, period. The essential self is eternal, it never changes. It is pure consciousness, and pure consciousness is timeless. Our normal experience of the passing of time is derived from change, the cycles of day and night, and the passing of thoughts. In deep meditation, when all awareness of things has ceased and the mind is completely still, there is no experience of change, and nothing by which to mark the passing of time. Time as we know it disappears. There is simply now. The essential self is beyond time and space. When we consider the nature of pure consciousness, time and space disappear.

The impression that your consciousness exists at a particular place in the world is an illusion. Everything we experience in this world is an illusion. Everything we experience is a construct within consciousness. Our sense of being a unique self is merely another construct of the mind. We place this image of the self at the center of our perceived world, giving us the sense of being in the world. But the truth is just the opposite, it is all within us. You have no location in space, you are space.

Quiet the Mind Exercise:

This is an exercise to quiet the mind. When the mind is troubling you, or the future is worrying you, or your mind is full of mental noise, or when you feel that you are not in the present moment. Sit still, clear your mind and put all of your attention on two different body senses, like feeling the air going in and out of your nose as you are breathing, and feeling your lungs expand and contract, or feeling your abdomen rise and fall as you breathe. Keep all your attention on these two body senses. You may pick two different body senses if you wish. Just notice, be aware of, and feel the body senses. If your thoughts wander, just bring them back to your body senses. Putting your attention on two different body senses will quiet the mind and bring you into the present moment. Please do this exercise now for several minutes and use it in the future when you feel that your mind is full of mental noise, or you are not in the present moment, or if you feel like you are dispersed.

Be Still and Know

Be still and know that I am god. This is what others call the silence, also called stillness. So be still and know that I am god means, stop the mind, allow quiet stillness to enter, when this happens you are in touch with your true self, the god self within. Be still and know that

I am god also means, still the mind and know that the "I am" is your essential self, the pure consciousness that lies behind all experience, the supreme being, the source of all. Consciousness is the source and creator of everything we know.

Those wise ones who see that the consciousness within themselves is the same consciousness within all conscious beings, attain eternal peace. If we perceive life from the perspective that all we know is a construct of consciousness, everything changes. With this shift, whether or not we are at peace is no longer determined by what we have or do in the material world. We have created our perception of the world, we have given it all the meaning and value it has for us, and we are free to see it differently.

Breath

Deep breathing has a generally calming effect on the whole personality and body, reducing stress, nervous tension, and calming the body and mind.

Breathing Exercise:

This breathing exercise is called "Deep breathing". When people are angry, afraid, or upset, you will find that their breathing becomes irregular, rapid, shallow, and noisy. In states of relaxation breathing is quiet, slow, and deep. This is how breathing can be used to influence conditions we normally consider beyond our control. For this exercise you can sit down or lay down. Begin by relaxing, then take a good deep breath. Start observing your breath, and focus consciously on making it quieter, slower, and deeper. Do this for a few breaths and notice how you feel. Then try this for five or ten minutes. Do this exercise now and everyday this week, and anytime in the future when you feel that it is needed.

Meditation

Meditation is your way of staying connected to source, to god. Through meditation, man reaches the state wherein he is always calm, never restless, where motion ceases, and god begins. This is be still and know that I am god. Meditation opens wide all the closed doors of your body, mind, and soul to admit the surge of god's power. Meditation is a communion with god for the purpose of acquiring knowledge and power to manifest god as co creator of his universe.

Meditation Exercise:

This meditation exercise is called "Be still and know". Please do this meditation for five or ten minutes twice a day for the next week, in the morning when you first get up and again in the evening. You should quiet the mind, close your eyes, and be aware of your breathing. Your intention would be nothing more than being in this moment and being consciously aware of your breathing. While you are breathing, feel your connection to the universe, to everything there is, and feel your connection to god. Feel the universes energy flowing through you. Focus on your breath, feeling your connection, and feeling the universes energy. By doing this I am saying, here I am, in a state of allowing source energy to flow purely through me. Five or ten minutes of effort will change your life. It will allow the energy that is natural to you to flow, you will feel better in the moment, and you will feel more energized when you come out of it.

Feelings and Emotions

We have been taught to live in fear from most of the people we have encountered during our life. When you feel fear, put it aside, it means you are living in the past or future, not in the now, not in the present moment. Become a being who thinks only of that which he is wanting, who speaks only that which he is wanting, who does only that which he is wanting, and therefore brings forth only joyful emotions and experiences. People are disturbed not by things, but by the view they take of them. Anytime you experience an upsetting situation, remember that if the negative is present, so must the positive and desirable outcome also be present. Most of us have created a fear based reality, so we do not get what we want. Fear is the energy which contracts, closes in, closes down, hides, and harms. Our energy sphere keeps contracting as we feel things like jealousy, blame, self justification, anger, fear, or the need to run away. This is what causes depression. Until we are willing to change, we are stuck. We should be creating our reality based on love. Love is the energy which expands, opens up, moves out, shares, and heals.

Worry, Fear, and Doubt

It has been said people age more by worry than by work. What is "worry"? It is the process of repeating the same train of thought over and over again with small alterations, coming to no result. It is the continued reproduction of thought forms, initiated by the mind and imposed on the consciousness. The thinker has dwelt on a painful subject. Replace the worry thought with a positive thought. Monitor your thoughts, if any negative thoughts enter your mind, change them at once to positive thoughts. You can train yourself to do this. Let go of things like worry, fear, doubt, and disappointment. Disease is the result of living in disharmony. Anger, anxiety, frustration, disappointment, worry, fear, doubt, and stress create thought forms that break down the physical body and make us sick.

Throughout our lives we pick up negative forms of energy, such as worry, fear, doubt, guilt, anger, judgment, criticism, blame, sorrow, and others. Negative energy can also be directed at us from other people (consciously or unconsciously). Things like worry, fear, and doubt are negative vibrations. Perfection in a human being means freedom from pain, suffering, worry, fear, doubt, and other negative emotions. Belief in limitation is the one and only thing that causes limitation. Doubt paralyzes us and leads to mistakes and inaction. Doubt freezes the will and makes a person ineffective. When your mind is in doubt, you must turn your thought toward the divine force. Such things as worry, fear, doubt, guilt, anger, judgment, criticism, blame, and sorrow will hold us down.

We have been taught to live in fear. Stress is fear. All human action and reaction originates in either love or fear. Most people operate in or from fear. We have a choice in life of either expanding or contracting our power. Anything positive, creative, or filled with love is expanding your energy. Anything negative, destructive, or filled with hate and anger is contracting your energy. Often we choose to contract or suppress our creative energy, and then we become afraid to take action. We always have the power of choice. We can expand, or we can contract. We can expand and radiate positive energy, or we can contract and collapse on ourselves, whether we call that contraction worry, fear, doubt, guilt, anger, judgment, criticism, blame, or sorrow.

Things like worry, fear, doubt, guilt, anger, judgment, criticism, blame, sorrow, and other characteristics of ego effect our vibration and what we radiate. Allowing is simply the absence of negative vibrations and things like doubt are a negative vibration. A negative vibration will delete and cancel the positive vibration of your desire. Think of yourself as a giant magnet and whatever you are feeling, whether it be love, happiness, joy, or fear, anger, and hate, you are creating and projecting a magnetic force that attracts to you the events, conditions and circumstances which are in direct correlation to what you are feeling. If you feel love, you will attract more love. If you will fear, you will attract more fear.

When you are consumed by emotions like fear, when your attention is on the things which are going wrong in your life, then in the best case you create inactivity and boredom, in the worst case, you create the things you fear and they will happen to you. We tend to avoid creating miracles by living life through our fears and other negative emotions. As you create your new reality, doubts and fears will present themselves. When our motivation is based in fear, we move away from what we want rather than toward what we do want. Most of us have created a fear based reality, so we do not get what we want. Hence the statement, that which I feared has come upon me. The only way to deal with insecurity, fear, and suffering is to live in the present moment in a positive and profound way.

Worry, fear, doubt and all other negative emotions are all low vibrational energies and low vibrational activities. To worry, fear and doubt is to create the negative situation. These are all negative creations. When you fill your mind with worry, fear and doubt you create the thing or situation not wanted. Creating something positive is always easier than creating something negative. The universe always supports positive creation.

Feelings and Emotions Exercise:

This exercise will help you deal with fear or help you if you are feeling fearful. If you are fearful, don't waste time trying to kill out fear. Instead, cultivate the quality of courage, and fear will disappear. This is similar to turning on a light to illuminate a dark room, instead of fighting the darkness. So when you feel fearful find the opposite quality which is courage. Fill your entire mind with courage, fill your entire being with courage, and hold on to this feeling of courage for as long as you can. The courage replaces the fear. Try this exercise now, pick something that recently made you feel fearful and use the opposite quality on it. You should also use this in the future anytime you feel fearful.

Affirmations

Every word you think and every word you speak is an affirmation. The tools are your thoughts, your speech, and your beliefs. Your beliefs are merely habitual thinking patterns that you have learned. You need to pay attention to your thoughts and what you say. Change the way you think and talk. Our thoughts, our speech, and our beliefs create our experiences. The more you choose to think thoughts that make you feel good, the quicker the affirmation works. Doing affirmations is choosing to think or say certain thoughts that will create positive results in the future.

Affirmation statements are going beyond the reality of the present into the creation of the future through the words you use in the now.

When you say I am prosperous, you are planting seeds for future prosperity. Affirmations should also start with words like "I have" or "I am" or "Thank you" and should be stated as if you already have the thing you desire. The universe takes your thoughts and words very literally and gives you what you say you want, always. It is very important to always maintain a positive, bright, and happy attitude. This helps your affirmations. Every thought you think counts, and everything you say counts. So watch carefully your thoughts and what you say. Remember the positive thought diet where we changed all our thoughts to positive creative thoughts for an entire day. Positive thoughts and speech bring good things into your life and of course negative thoughts and speech brings bad things into your life. When you change your thinking process, everything in your life will also change. You'll be amazed and delighted to see how people, places, things, and circumstances can change.

When you feel that you're stuck in some situation, or when your affirmations aren't working, it usually means that there's more forgiveness work to be done. When you don't flow freely with life in the present moment, it usually means that you are holding on to the past or a past moment. It can be regret, sadness, hurt, fear, guilt, blame, anger, resentment, or sometimes even revenge. Let these go and come to the present moment. Only in the present moment can you create your future. If you are doing positive affirmations and not getting results, check to see how often during the day you feel bad or upset. These are most likely delaying the manifestations of your affirmations and stopping the flow. When this happens use one of the exercises in this book to change your thoughts and feelings. Affirmations provide you with positive statements to replace negative messages that undermine your health and life. Affirmations only work if you make statements of things you know to be true, not want to be true.

As part of the meditation, you can repeat affirmations, positive suggestions stated consciously with the intention of changing negative thought patterns into more beneficial ones. An affirmation is a statement of gratitude. Like "Thank you god for the money I have in my bank account". Incorporate gratitude and thankfulness into your everyday life. Make "I am" statements, like "I am loving", or "I am successful", etc. Say these to yourself over and over. Example: "I am prosperous, I deserve to be prosperous". When making affirmations, be specific, positive, passionate, and present, in the present moment. Our subconscious accepts everything we say as true. It does not distinguish between truth and fiction. Thus the saying: "We become what we think about". Another saying is "As above, so below". Stand in front of a mirror and say these affirmations to yourself. Affirmation statements especially with frequent repetition, create a blue print for success. When you are making affirmations, the mind is stopped and it can not fill your head with mental noise. This is a good way to quiet the mind, as it must focus on your affirmations.

Periodically say to yourself, "What am I thinking, would I like this thought to create my life, would I like to have the experience that this thought could bring to me". Make positive statements about your life, let these statements become a habit. What do you want to have, do, or be? Now get into the feeling of having already accomplished it. You must assume the feeling of that intention already fulfilled.

Sample affirmations:

I am thankful for all that is positive in my life.
I allow my highest good to come to me now.
I am in love.
I radiate love, and love fills my life.
I am involved in a loving, committed relationship.
I love and appreciate my body.
I am healthy and full of energy.
I am open to receiving.
I live in a loving, abundant, harmonious universe, and
I am grateful.
Money flows into my life in an abundant way.
My income is constantly increasing.
I have a steady flow of money into my life.
I am a magnet for money.
I delight in the financial security that is a constant in
my life.
Thank you god for the money I have in my bank account.

Mind

When you wrap your thoughts around your desire, sharpen your focus, and feel expectancy, you more easily draw the desired object or situation to you. Your desire for something sets in motion the energetic resonance of attraction. Your thoughts about that desire intensify the resonance. From the spiritual perspective, thoughts are energetic vibrations that exist outside the physical body. Learning to control your thoughts is one of the key criteria of becoming conscious in your manifestations. When you begin to truly understand the power of thoughts, you'll realize that becoming conscious of how you expend your mental energy is vital to creating the life you want.

Mind Exercise:

Make up, or create several affirmations that you can use for this exercise. Your affirmations should be positive "I am" or "I have" or "Thank you" statements about things you want in your life. Then I would like you to say these affirmations several times out loud by standing in front of a mirror. After that you can say them to yourself. Do this for several minutes. You can also say these affirmations to yourself often throughout the day. Note, you do not have to be in front of a mirror. You should use affirmations often in your life to help create your life.

Gratitude

Gratitude is a spiritual practice of faith and expectation in action, and it is a very important component in the manifestation of what you desire in your life. Gratitude is a very high vibrational energy, so when you practice it often, it will expand the good in your life. Gratitude is one of the most powerful energies in the universe because it offers so many benefits. Gratitude attracts what we want. The universal law of attraction says that we will attract into our life the things we think about and focus on.

Have the attitude of gratitude. Count your blessings and think often of all the good in your life. Say "Thank You" often during the day. Contemplate the areas of your life that are working well. Asking for something comes from lack, always give gratitude for something. When you thank god in advance for something you wish to experience in your reality you acknowledge that it is already there. Thankfulness is the most powerful statement to god. One should always incorporate gratitude and thankfulness into your everyday life. You should be grateful for the things you have and the things you want. Gratitude is an expression of love. When you feel grateful you are giving love. Say thank you often. An affirmation is a statement of gratitude. Like "Thank you god for the money I have in my bank account". Incorporate gratitude and thankfulness into your everyday life. Gratitude for the abundance you have received is the best assurance that the abundance will continue.

When you are thankful and appreciative for everything you experience, you will open the door to draw into your life countless miracles. By regularly expressing gratitude, you will stop focusing on the negative circumstances in your life. When we consciously practice being grateful for the people, situations, and abundance in our lives we begin to attract better relationships, better situations, and more abundance. Practice gratitude everyday so that it becomes automatic and second nature to you.

When you are in a sincere state of gratitude your energy and vibrational level is one of acceptance and harmony. You vibrate at a much higher vibrational frequency which is exactly what attracts to you the people, situations, and abundance that you desire. Think of yourself as a giant magnet and whatever you are feeling, whether it be love, happiness, joy, or fear, anger, and hate, you are creating and projecting a magnetic force that attracts to you the events, conditions and circumstances which are in direct correlation to what you are feeling. If you feel love, you will attract more love. If you feel fear, you will attract more fear. Expressing gratitude for any situation projects a magnetic force that draws to you more of what you are expressing gratitude for. So practice giving thanks for everything everyday.

Feelings and Gratitude Exercise:

This exercise is called "Feelings and Gratitude". Using the affirmations from the previous exercise, say them this time with lots of positive feelings and lots of gratitude. I would like you to say these affirmations several times out loud by standing in front of a mirror, but this time say them with lots of positive feelings and lots of gratitude. After that you can say them to yourself with lots of positive feelings and lots of gratitude. Do this for several minutes. Repeat these affirmations with lots of positive feelings and lots of gratitude many times over the next week.

Feeling is the language of the soul. The things we do, create the feelings in our body, and the feeling is the prayer. Feeling is a lost language that speaks to our soul. So, we must feel what we want. Feel compassion and gratitude for what you want.

White Light

When you are in the deepest part of your being, as a single point of consciousness glowing with intelligence, you experience white light. This is because white light comes from and represents this deepest part of yourself and it can be used for cleansing and releasing all that is not you. You can do this by filling yourself with your own white light, and returning to the consciousness you know and recognize as yourself when you are in balance. When you fill yourself with white light, and surround yourself with white light, you will feel protected, you feel safe, and you will feel more relaxed. When you relax more, and open more, you glow with more white light and feel protected. This process continues until you are totally open, totally relaxed, feeling totally protected, and completely in white light.

Holistic healers refer to white light as part of the universe that stores all positive energy. By calling on the white light, it is believed that the human energy field or aura, can be cleansed and protected from negative energy. Negativity in any form can be damaging to the human energy field or aura. Fear, anger, depression, negative people and places, and arguments can actually create negative energy that will cling to you or build up in your home and cause problems over time. To cleanse your home, just fill your home with white light. Spiritual cleansing is very important for yourself and your home. I recommend that this be done periodically, more if you find yourself feeling stressed or fatigued. Spiritual Protection is something that everyone should know how to do.

White Light Exercise:

This is a white light shower exercise. When you take a shower, see the water cleansing you and washing away all negative energy and replacing it with positive energy, beautiful white light, and love energy. The negative energy is flowing out of you and down the drain. In this exercise we are washing away all negative energy and replacing it positive energy, beautiful white light, and love energy. Then surround yourself with love and white light to keep all negative things from touching and affecting you. Really focus on seeing it clearly in your mind, and keep building it up so it's super bright and glowing. See it as a solid barrier of protection that negativity cannot cross. Do not rush the shower, enjoy it and feel your energy changing, feel the love and light entering your body, your being. Do this white light shower exercise everyday this week and when you feel you need it in the future. You could do this white light shower exercise every time you take a shower. If you do not have a shower, take a white light bath. Fill the bath with water and see the water as beautiful white light. Get in the tub so most of your body is under water and see the white light water dissolving all the negative energy in your body and replacing it with positive energy, beautiful white light, and love energy.

Additional Helpful Information –
Change the Way You Feel

This exercise is called change the way you feel. Do this exercise now and anytime in the future when you wish to change the way you feel. If your not feeling good and you want to change the way you feel, or if you want to lift good feelings higher, take a few minutes and go through a mental list of everything you love and adore and are thankful for, the effect in your life will be amazing. As you are going through the list of things you love and adore and are thankful for, feel the love and thankfulness for each thing on your list. You can also make a written list of the things you love and adore and are thankful for. When you change the way you feel, you are on a different frequency, and the law of attraction responds instantaneously. On any one day you can change the future through the way you feel.

CHAPTER

We are Slaves to the Material World

We are slaves to the material world. Why? Because man likes to build things that require constant maintenance. A house, a yard, and a car are good examples of this. We are always fixing or improving our house. It needs a paint job, or a new floor, or a new bathroom, and the house needs constant cleaning. The lawn needs mowing every week, the bushes need trimming, and the driveway needs sweeping. The same for our car, it needs periodic oil changes, tune ups, and maintenance. You have to check the air pressure in the tires. You have to keep the car washed and waxed. We are always taking care of and fixing things in the material world. Our main focus is on having things in the material world, only to use much of our time or all of our time to keep these things in good repair and working properly. Unfortunately, man creates things that need constant maintenance and that do not last. Sadly, the reason behind this is mostly due to money, as business wants us to pay for repeated repairs and maintenance. The world, or business wants you to spend your money to fix things and replace things, so things are not built to last. If we built things to last and that did not need constant repair, we would have much more free time and money to do other things.

We also spend much of our time running errands and going shopping. I know people who use all of their free time running errands and going shopping. I have a relative who uses most of their free time running errands and then complains about never having any free time, and yet if they have an afternoon off, they always find some errand to run.

Many of us are also slaves to the nine to five job and will be for most of our lives. Once again, man has created the situation where we need to spend much of our time at work, usually at the employers location. So we spent time driving to work, spent time at work, and driving home from work. For most of us this is a largest part of everyday.

All of our modern technology is one more thing that is enslaving us to the material world. We have instant information and communication with others, and this takes up much of our time and energy. I see people who are so attached to this modern technology that it consumes most of their free time and energy. While modern technology can be very helpful, anything in excess can be harmful. Due to modern technology many people are plugged in and tuned out, meaning they are so connected to this instant information and communication that they are not even aware of what is going on around them in the physical world, much less the spiritual world. I have had people run into me with their shopping cart because they were so focused on their phone and were not paying attention to their physical surroundings. This is a person plugged into technology and tuned out from the world.

Most of us are so busy doing our routine things, like working, shopping, running errands, cleaning the house, mowing the lawn, washing the car, and others, that we never really have any free time to pursue or accomplish our dreams and our goals. The trick is to make time to do the things we really care about and not worry so much about the routine things. If we cut back on some of the routine things or do them less often, no real harm is done, it only means we will do the routine things less often, and have more time to pursue our hopes, wishes, goals, and dreams. Someone once said insanity is doing the same thing over and over, expecting a different result.

Goals

Deciding what goals to pursue, that's sometimes a tough question. Don't weigh ideas or wonder, don't doubt your direction or depend on others to tell you what you should or shouldn't do. Go toward what touches your heart. Ask yourself what's worth the effort and sacrifices that come with commitment to any goal. People rarely ever fail, they only stop trying. It's better to make a mistake with the full force of your being, than to timidly avoid mistakes with a trembling spirit. I know people who are so cautious that they will never step out of their comfort zone and thus will never see any of their dreams fulfilled. To much caution is really fear, and when you fear you attract what you fear to you. Hence the statement, that which I feared has come upon me. The road to happiness is always under construction, the journey never ends. Focus on taking life one step at a time until you get it right, set aside those things you can do later. Focus on what you need to do now to reach your goals. You must work toward your goals step by step, hour by hour. So the plan is to make the most of your days, of your time. You can cry about your past mistakes or you can live well this day, and create the future you desire.

It is really important to be specific in setting goals. You have to be specific, because the universe will deliver what you want, that's how the universe works. If you are not specific what you get may not be exactly what you want. Use your mind to see your goal and use your feelings to experience your goal. Setting goals is like delegating to your universal manager or spirit what you are creating in your life.

Realize you have a purpose. In order to discover our purpose or creative intention, we must believe and trust that a creative intelligence is seeking to create through us. You must have a definite purpose. You must make up your mind as to what you want and where you want to go. You must keep your goal or dream in your mind often so the universe can deliver. However, you must also take action. Remember the three levels of creation are thoughts, words, and action. What do

I want to do today to make me happy. What do I want to do today to achieve my goals.

Purpose/Goal:
Do I have a major purpose/goal?

1. What plans do I have to accomplish my purpose/goal?
2. How much time per day should I devote to my plan to accomplish my purpose/goal?
3. How often should I work on this plan?

Is your purpose/goal a burning obsession or a burning desire?

1. How do I spend my time?
2. On pleasure or working on my purpose/goal?
3. Do you use your free time to work on your purpose/goal?

Learn to live in the now. Don't worry about yesterday and don't worry about tomorrow, learn to live for today, live in the now. Make the most of everyday by doing what you want to do. Think of life like a class room and we are learning how to live.

Setting Life Goals, the six major areas are:

1. Career – What do you want to accomplish as far as your career is concerned?
2. Financial – Realistically, how much money do you want to have and how will you get it?
3. Physical – What program for physical fitness and health do you want to develop?
4. Mental – In what areas of your life do you wish to study and obtain more knowledge?
5. Family – What relationships do you want to have and maintain with your family and friends?
6. Spiritual – What are you striving for spiritually?

Set your goals with a vision of the new and improved you. Don't get caught up in the trap of living in the past. Recognize your current reality and then move on. All we have to do is decide what to do with the time that is given to us. This is very important, decide, it is your creation.

Use your time wisely. Don't let the time use you, use the time for your own benefit. What did you accomplish this week, month, year, etc. Get the important things done, by doing so, you are in the light, and source will guide you. Write down your top goals and top priorities. Then work only on these, using your time wisely. You can spend your time or waste your time. People who fail to achieve their real desires in life do so because they major in minor things, they use all of their time on non important routine things. Remember, there is no fate, but what we make for ourselves.

Goals Exercise:

This is an exercise to set long term goals, medium term goals, and short term goals for each of the six major areas in life. For each long term goal, you should have several related medium term goals, and each medium term goal should have several related short term goals. So each long term goal is broken down into medium term goals, and each medium term goal is further broken down into short term goals.

Using these six major areas:

1. Career – What do you want to accomplish as far as your career is concerned?
2. Financial – Realistically, how much money do you want to have and how will you get it?
3. Physical – What program for physical fitness and health do you want to develop?
4. Mental – In what areas of your life do you wish to study and obtain more knowledge?
5. Family – What relationships do you want to have and maintain with your family and friends?
6. Spiritual – What are you striving for spiritually?

Part one is to write three or four long term goals for each of the six major areas. A long term goal is something you wish to complete in the next year or two or more depending on what the goal is. You should have several long term goals, for each major areas. If you make too many long term goals at one time, you most likely will not find the time to work on them. So, a few long term goal for each major area is enough for now.

Next I want you to pick the most important long term goal for each major area. So you should end up with six long term goals, one for each of the six major areas.

Part two is to write several (not to many, three or four should do) medium term goals for each of the six major areas, or for each of the six long term goals. A medium term goal is something you wish to complete in the next month or two or three. These medium term goals should relate to and support the long term goals listed above. So a medium term goal is a long term goal broken down into several steps or tasks.

Part three is to write several (not to many, three or four should do) short term goals for each of the medium term goals you created for the six long term goals. A short term goal is something you wish to complete in the next week or two or three. These should relate to and support the long term goals and medium term goals listed above. So a short term goal is each medium term goal broken down into several smaller steps or tasks.

Remember, for each of your six long term goals, you should have several related medium term goals, and each medium term goal should have several related short term goals. So each long term goal is broken down into medium term goals, and each medium term goal is further broken down into short term goals. Of course these medium term goals and short term goals must support the long term goal.

After you have written up your long term goals, medium term goals, and short term goals, I want you to pick the one long term goal that is the most important to you. This is the goal you should work on first. Remember this is the most important goal. I want you to make a plan to start working on the short term goals that support the medium term goals that support the long term goal. Make a plan to work on these every day or every week or every month. If you do not start working on these items, they will never come into your life. Remember, you must take action, you must do something. You can major in minor things or you can accomplish your goals, the choice is yours. Sometimes it is easier to pick the most important long term goal and work only on that one goal, so you do not spread yourself to thin. That is what you are going to do. We are going to work only on the most important long term goal.

Use your time wisely. What did you accomplish this week, month, year, etc. Get the important thing done, by doing so, you are in the light, and source will guide you. Write down your top goals and top priorities. Then work only on these by using your time wisely.

Remember, most of us are failing by not doing, by letting things happen in our lives, instead of directing our lives and determining our outcome. It is better to have tried and failed, then to have failed to try. If we get caught up in the small day to day busy stuff, we could miss our chance to give the commitment needed to achieve the greater things in life. People who fail to achieve their real desires in life do so because they major in minor things.

We do things and don't even know why we do these things. For most of us life is just one big habit or routine, we wake up in the morning, wash ourselves, eat breakfast, drive to work, do our daily work functions, drive home after work, make dinner, eat dinner, watch the television for several hours, and then finally we go to sleep. And we repeat this process at least five days a week, and of course weekends may be slightly different. So, at the end of our lives we realize we have done the same thing over and over without accomplishing our goals.

So start working on your goals. Make a plan to spend a certain amount of time every day and every week on these goals. Of course you should start working on the short term goals first, but also allocate some time for the medium term goals and the long term goal. If you use all of your time washing your car, at the end of a year you will have a very clean car. If you use some of your time on your goals, at the end of a year you will have one or more completed goals. Which would make you happier, a clean car, or several completed goals? Now, I am not saying you should never wash your car, that would be silly, but maybe you could wash it less often or only when it's really needed. Using this goals exercise is how I was able to write this book, and in the end I was very happy that I accomplished this long term goal. It was well worth the time and effort.

When you complete your long term goal, you should do this exercise again. This will allow you to create a new list of goals, as our goals change with the passing of time. Once again you would pick the most important long term goal and work only on that goal. Then each time you complete a goal just do this exercise again to pick the next long term goal to work on. By using this method, you are always working on the most important long term goal and not wasting time on less important goals.

Results

Your life is created first in your mind and then in the world. Write down what you want, this way you give the universe instructions to produce certain results. When you are clear, what you want will show up in your life, but only to the extent that you are clear. Deal with situations which must be dealt with, and don't dwell on anything which does not support what you choose to create. When you are consumed by fear, when your attention is on the things which are going wrong in your life, then in the best case you create inactivity and boredom, in the worst case, you create the things you fear and they will happen to you. Become conscious of where you are putting your attention, then you are aware of what you are creating. If your not happy with what you are creating, you can begin now creating consciously something better. Forget your worries, forget your fears, in place of them, visualize the conditions you would like to see. Realize their availability, declare to yourself that you already have all these things that you desire, that your needs have been met. Believe that ye receive it, and ye shall have it.

You have no idea what your capable of. From the moment we wake, we should devote ourselves to the perfection of whatever we do. We need discipline. We are all moving closer to death, so we should enjoy life in every breath, in everything we do. The smart man has a definite schedule and follows it. He does today the things that need doing today.

Abundance

Abundance is a feeling. Become more abundant and attract more money. Feel abundant as often and as long as possible. Do you feel abundant? You do not have to actually be abundant in order to attract abundance, but you do have to feel abundant. Any feeling of lack of abundance causes a resistance that does not allow abundance.

Remember a situation of abundance, if you catch yourself wallowing in a bad memory or engaged in bad thinking, call up a contrasting memory in which you have felt rich, beautiful, accomplished, capable or whatever state of being you desire. When you get past self doubt, abundance flows naturally, almost without effort.

Try this wallet abundance process. Hold a $100 bill in your wallet. Do no spend it. But mentally spent the $100 bill 20 to 30 times in a day. You will receive the vibrational feeling advantage of having spent $2,000 to $3,000 everyday.

Seemingly magical things will begin to occur as soon as you achieve that wonderful feeling of financial abundance. The money you are currently earning will seem to go further and unexpected amounts of money in various increments will begin to show up in your life. You have to feel good about great abundance before you will allow the pleasure of great abundance to flow into your life.

Gratitude for the abundance you have received is the best insurance that the abundance will continue.

The essence of this law is that you must think abundance, see abundance, feel abundance, believe in abundance, and give thanks for your abundance. Let no thought of limitation enter your mind. If you only hold up a glass, you only get a glass full, even if an ocean of abundance should rain down on you.

True abundance has nothing to do with anything that I am having and everything to do with what I am being. Abundance is something to be, not something to do. When you share your abundance of beingness abundantly with all those whose lives you touch, everything you want will come to you automatically. He's being joy, love, compassion, wisdom, and humor. He's being one, which is the highest level of being. Abundance is a state of being, a state of mind. Your job is to create the vibration around your desire and the intention and to stay in harmonious alignment with the law. The higher your level of emotion and belief, the higher your vibration. The higher your vibration, the more swiftly you'll attract into your life the abundance, prosperity, and other things you desire. Self limiting thoughts or doubt, slow or block the arrival of your goals. Keep your energy and emotions high.

Money

Everyone has exactly as much money as they expect and allow themselves to have. Those who strongly believe in their capacity for creating wealth will continually make money. So in regards to money, you should really create this, think this, feel this, and believe that the money is yours. Many people make the mistake of running after money first, instead of first seeking happiness. To try to earn money with a disgruntled, worried mind is not only unsuccessful, but it produces more anxiety and unhappiness. Earning money with a serene and happy attitude leads not only to success but ensures happiness also.

Conjure up images that cause you to offer a vibration that allows money. Your goal is to create images that feel good to you. The goal is to find the feeling place of what it would feel like to have enough money rather than finding the feeling place of what it would feel like to not have enough money. What about creating a very positive current of financial abundance. What about getting so good at visualizing that the money flows to and through you easily.

When you change the way you feel about money, the amount of money in your life will change. The better you feel about money, the more money you magnetize to yourself. Imagine that you are wealthy right now. Imagine that you have all the money you need right now. How would you feel if you had all the money you needed and plenty more. You would be relaxed and have peace of mind, you would be happy. That's the feeling you want to capture now.

Success

Poverty is unnatural, it is man made through the limits man puts upon himself. Joyless work, small pay, no future, nothing to look forward to, god never planned such an existence. It is man made and you can be man enough to unmake it as far as you are concerned. There is no philosophy which will help a man to succeed when he is always doubting his ability to do so, and thus attracting failure. When we analyze a lack of success in any aspect of our lives, we tend to look outside ourselves for the explanation. Often the answer is that we are getting in our own way. We all work against ourselves most of the time.

If your procrastination is the result of fear, put the fear aside, risk failure. Put fear aside by telling yourself that while you may fail if you make the move you desire, your failure is certain and automatic if you don't make the move. If you procrastinate when faced with a big difficult problem, analyze, break the problem into parts, and handle one part at a time. All factors of success or failure are in your inner world. You make your own inner world, and through it your outer world. How can you develop will? Choose some objective that you think you can not accomplish, and then try with all your might to do that one thing. When you have achieved success, go on to something bigger. The key to success is to have dominant thought patterns that are totally aligned with what you want. Success is not final and failure is not fatal, but it is the courage to continue on that counts.

Self discipline is the channel through which all your power must flow. Think of your mind as a reservoir where you have been storing up potential power. You must learn to release that power in precise quantities and in specific directions. You must regulate this power and maintain control over it. Enforced self discipline is controlling your emotions, taking control of your mind, having a positive mental attitude, and controlled enthusiasm. Enthusiasm is one of the missing pieces of the law of success. I have noticed that when I have enthusiasm for just one thing, then all other things seem to go better. So try to find at least one thing to be enthusiastic about. I have also noticed that when all areas of your life seem bad, it is hard to find enthusiasm. Then you must change something or do something or add something so you can bring enthusiasm back into your life.

Success is absolutely the amount of joy you feel. Success is about a happy life and a happy life is just a string of happy moments. Success, happiness, and good luck are available to any of us who are ready for it. Unfortunately, most of us do not know how to unlock the door. We sit and wait for our life to change, never realizing that the door to the prison is open. There are no guards. You may not be aware of it, but your attitude is either the key to open the door or the lock on the door. This is the door to fulfillment.

Work

Someone once told me that their definition of work is anytime you do something, but would rather be doing something else. For most people work is just that, doing something we don't want to do to earn money to compensate us for the time spent so that we can do or buy things that we want or need. To me, happiness is loving what you do and getting someone to pay you to do it. What motivates you to work everyday? Is it survival, security, tradition, prestige, power, or success? Is it creativity and fulfillment? The real problem we face is that we are trading our total life energy every single day. There is nothing in your life more valuable then the time you have left. You cannot put too much attention and importance on the way you invest those moments.

Since we will consume a portion of our total life energy for money, we must decide on how that money will be used. There is nothing wrong with having money. The manner in which you earn and spend the money is what matters here. If you acquire your money doing something you love to do and manage to help others in the process, the expenditure of your life energy was in proportion to what you received. If you spend more than you earned on things you don't need or try to buy happiness or impress other people, you are in big trouble. If you get your money through activities that are illegal or harmful to other people, you are heading down the path to a lower vibrational existence which can only make circumstances in your life worst and hinder your spiritual growth.

Money means freedom. Instead of buying things, use your money to buy time. You may have an unlimited amount of money someday, but you will not have an unlimited amount of time. The only way is to buy time to do what you love to do. If you earn money doing what you love to do, you will never work another day in your life and you will have enough money to pay others to do what they excel at. Instead of repairing your own house, fixing your own car, cleaning your own house, or mowing your own lawn, find people who have achieved excellence in these areas and pay them to do it, and do it well. By achieving excellence in your chosen field or occupation, you will have more than enough money to pay others to do things you do not wish to do or are not good at. If you are a painter, you can use your time to paint, or you can use your time mowing the lawn, or you could pay someone else to mow the lawn giving you the time to paint and do what you really enjoy. This is buying time. If we love what we do, we can achieve excellence. Achieving excellence is the key to life long prosperity.

Two factors occur when you are doing what you love. One, you are motivated because you are fulfilling your passion and two, because your work is a pleasure, it seems like you are making a living without working. We can automatically be motivated by the inner drive of our passion which makes everything we do seem effortless. When our passion is fulfilled, we put our heart into our work. Do not worry about making a living, true masters are those who have chosen to make a life, rather than a living. Do whatever you love, do nothing else. You have so little time, how can you think of wasting a moment doing something for a living that you don't like to do, that is not a living, that is dying.

Breath

When doing breath work, keep your tongue in the yogic position, touch the tip of the tongue to the root of your mouth. Yoga philosophy teaches that there are two nerve currents of opposite polarity in the human body, which begin and end at points in the roof of the mouth, when you make that connection with the tongue, it is said that you are completing a circuit and keeping the energy of breath within instead of dissipating it to the outside.

Breathing Exercise:

This breathing exercise is called "Universe breath". Please do this exercise everyday this week. You can do this exercise laying down if you like. Close your eyes. Begin by observing your breath. Now imagine that each time you inhale, you are not doing it, the universe is blowing air into you, and each time you exhale, you are not doing it, the universe is withdrawing air from you. Try to picture yourself as the passive recipient of breath. As the universe breathes into you and expands your lungs, chest, and abdomen, let yourself feel the breath penetrating to every part of your body, even your fingers and your toes. See if you can do this for at least ten breath cycles, then increase it to several minutes.

Meditation Exercise:

The manifestation symbol of god is Om. This is the Om mantra technique. One should meditate on this word, contemplating and surrendering to it. Meditation on Om results in cosmic consciousness and the removal of all mental and physical obstacles to success on the spiritual path. As you exhale chant Om (O-o-o-o-o-m-m-n). Let it flow out easily, chant it quietly several times. Then after a while mentally chant Om going still more deeply within, while listening in the inner ear canals to any subtle sounds that may be discerned. If you can actually hear a subtle continuous sound in your ears as though pervading your field of awareness, give your attention to that. Then cease mental chanting while continuing to listen to the mental sound resonating in your field of awareness, give attention to this sound. Please do this meditation twice a day for the entire week, in the morning when you first get up and again in the evening. For ten or fifteen minutes twice everyday, you should quiet the mind, close your eyes, and chant Om (O-o-o-o-o-m-m-n). Please use this meditation for the entire week.

Feelings and Emotions

When we perceive our lives to be on an inevitable path of continual decline, when we think that our situations are impossible and that we are failures, the likely response is to resign our lives to problems and thereby creating more problems. You shouldn't blame yourself when a series of things go wrong all at once. If you do, you will surely conclude that you are the victim of bad luck and therefore you are an unlucky person. The solution is to accept it, go with it, and then get rid of it. Changing the impossible to the possible is a matter of letting go of destructive patterns that restrict any aspect of our lives. Such things as worry, fear, doubt, guilt, anger, blame, regret, and addictions can hold us down. As we try to move forward we find it impossible because the weights of negativity are almost unbearable. The bottom line is that our thoughts create our reality. If we are focused on the negative or the impossible, our subconscious will direct us to people, places, and circumstances to prove that we are right. In order to preserve itself, the subconscious always seeks to prove that what we are thinking is in fact true. If you think that every time you get into a relationship the person will leave you, that becomes your reality. Your subconscious then searches for people to come into your life to fulfill that perception. To destroy an undesirable rate of mental vibration, concentrate upon the opposite pole to that which you desire to suppress.

When life's outcomes do not match our wishes, we feel threatened. Our primary focus is on survival, so we are no longer focused on what we want, but on what we don't want. Our motivation is based in fear, and we move toward what we don't want rather than toward what we do want. Our energy sphere keeps contracting as we feel jealousy, blame, self justification, anger, fear, or the need to run away. This is what causes depression. Many of us have visited this dark place called depression. In this state, your only wish is to be allowed to give up your beliefs, your dreams, and the things you hold dear, as they all seem lost to you. Until we are willing to change, we are stuck. Every time we blame something outside of ourselves, we are in effect trying to weasel out of being accountable. Weasel statements are all wrapped around one basic belief which is, "I am not the cause, I am the effect". Said another way "I am the victim". When we refuse to take responsibility for where we are, we become imprisoned by our own thoughts. We are locked into the past and cannot escape into the future. Freedom comes when you stop placing responsibility on others for your happiness, success, or financial condition.

Feelings and Emotions Exercise:

This is called banish a negative quality. To banish a negative quality, concentrate upon the opposite quality, and the vibrations will gradually change from negative to positive. By changing your polarity you may master your moods, change your mental states, remake your disposition, and build up character. The mastery of polarity is the mastery of the mental transmutation or mental alchemy. Try this exercise now, pick a negative quality that you recently experienced or that you would like to change and use this exercise on it. You should also use this in the future anytime you have or notice a negative quality that you would like to change.

Body

Direct your attention into the body. Everything you'll ever need to know is within you. The secrets of the universe are imprinted on the cells of your body. But you haven't learned how to read the wisdom of the body. Your body like everything else in life is a mirror of our inner thoughts and beliefs. A relaxed mind gives a relaxed body. You must bring the body and the mind into active harmony with each other. You must recognize your kinship with the surrounding universe. Live each moment of everyday. We must live this moment in a deep way. Don't wait to start living. Your life should be real in this very moment. You can live every moment of everyday deeply, in touch with the wonders of life. Being in the here and now, the present, is the door to the kingdom of god. This will help transform your life and everything in it.

Present Moment Awareness Exercise:

For this exercise we will do a present moment awareness exercise. This will help you put your attention and awareness into the present moment or the now. Using the first item on the list "Your body", sit still and clear your mind, then put all of your attention on your body and hold it there. Putting your attention on your body will bring you into the present moment. Then feel the power, feel the love inside of yourself. Do this till you are in the now, in the present moment, and you feel better. For five minutes several times each day, practice getting present by putting your attention into one of the following or by performing one of the following. For instance, the last item "Physical exercise" is exactly what it states, just exercise for five minutes while keeping all of your attention and awareness on exercising. Several times each day for the entire week, try a different item, see which works best for you. Use these items or make up your own:

1. Your body
2. Be one with nature
3. A tree
4. Yourself
5. Your breath
6. Your heart beat
7. Really listen to someone
8. Take a bath or shower, feel the water
9. Physical exercise

When the past is troubling you or the future is worrying you, use this to put you back into the present moment, the now. This is an exercise to put you into present moment or the now, use it as needed.

Beauty Harmony and Love Exercise:

This is the beauty harmony and love exercise. Do this exercise for one hour. Go some place outdoors where you will not be disturbed for the entire hour. You could go to your back yard, or a park, or some other setting outdoors. The goal is to sit in nature for one hour. During this hour do not talk to anyone. For this exercise just sit there for one hour without talking and without interruption. During this hour look at things and see the beauty, see the harmony, and see the love in the things you look at. Look at one thing for a few minutes, then move on to another thing. Keep this up for the entire hour. Hold your attention on one thing while you consider how beautiful, harmonious, and loving it is. The longer you focus, the better you should feel. This will improve your mood and raise your vibrational level. Do this exercise once a week for the next few weeks. This exercise may take some effort. You may have to work yourself up to an hour. This is an exercise you should use whenever it is needed in the future.

Additional Helpful Information – When a Body Part Hurts

When a body part hurts, or you injure yourself, that injured body part goes out of communication with the rest of the body, which is part of the reason for the pain. Often body parts hurt when they are out of communication with the rest of your body. To handle this injured body part and put it back in communication with the rest of the body one should have physical contact with the injured body part for several minutes, several times a day until the pain is gone. So when you have a body part that hurts or is injured, rub, touch, and massage that body part, or any part of your body that hurts. So if you hurt your foot, rub, touch, and massage your foot for several minutes, several times a day until the pain is gone. The rubbing, touching, and massaging puts that hurt body part back in communication with the rest of the body, and the pain will eventually go away. If you have a sore body part, try this right now.

Use this technique in the future whenever you have a body part that hurts or you injure yourself.

If you have an actual physical or medical problem, you should always seek the help of a medical professional.

Additional Helpful Information – Headaches and Concentration

This exercise will help you get relief from headaches and will sharpen your concentration. When you get a headache, you can massage the point between the eyebrows, also known as the third eye or spiritual eye. Also, massage the point in the temples, the dip just beside the outer edge of the eyes, this sharpens concentration as well as easing headaches. Use this technique whenever you get a headache or when you wish to sharpen your concentration.

CHAPTER

What We Say

What we say can raise or lower our vibration. If we say kind and positive things to others and about others, we are raising our vibrational level and raising the vibrational level of the other person. If we say unkind and harmful things to others or about others, we are lowering our vibrational level and lowering the vibrational level of the other person. So what you say has much to do with our vibrational level and the vibrational level of those we come into contact with. Remember the one day positive thought diet, affirmations, and gratitude, or should I say the power of positive thinking. These are all operating from the point of positive statements, positive energy, and positive vibrations. So if you catch yourself in a conversation with someone and it starts to go negative, it is best to change the subject or use "Keep it sweet and friendly" to keep the conversation on a positive note so you do not lower your own vibrational level and the vibrational level of those around you. If you catch yourself saying something negative, simply stop what you are saying and think of something positive to say, or if you do not have anything positive to say, then say nothing. It is better to say nothing, than to say something negative. The negative comment will only cause harm and hurt someones feelings, which will most likely lead to future difficulties with that person.

You Get What You Give

Based on the law of attraction, you get back what you give or dish out, if you give love, you get back love, if you give anger, you get back anger, if you are a jerk to people, then people will be a jerk to you. So watch how people are talking to you and acting around you or reacting to you. This will help you determine if you are in a good state. If people are kind, helpful and loving to you, well then you are in a good state. However, if people are unkind, angry, and mean to you, then you should look at your state and see why you are attracting this into your experience. Perhaps an attitude change on your behalf is in order. Use one of the previous exercises in this book to change the way you think and feel. Remember it is your thoughts, your feelings, and vibrational state that is pulling experiences and situations into your life. If you are not happy with the experiences and situations that are coming to you, just change your thoughts, change your feelings, thus changing your vibrational state. And then your experiences and situations should also change.

I know a person who sometimes can be a complete jerk to other people. This person does not even realize that they are behaving badly, they think it is acceptable for them to behave this way. Sometimes people are a jerk back to this person, and this person is surprised and becomes greatly upset when the same behavior is directed back to them. I have heard them say things like "People are hard on me" or "People are always picking on me", well guess what, they are getting back exactly what they are giving out. I have tried to explain it to this person, but it does not register, they just think that I am also picking on them, so I have stopped trying. Sadly, this will keep happening until this person stops being a jerk to others. I have a relative who is angry all of the time, and always has negative comments to say to everyone, and likes to start fights with anyone and everyone. Of course no one likes this person due to their bad disposition. This person has often commented to me that they do not understand why other people do not like them. Sadly, no one will ever like this person as long as they have that angry attitude and bad disposition.

Respect and Consideration of Others

You should have and show respect to others. Even if a person is in a bad state, or at a very low vibrational level. You do not know what has happened to this person and why they are at a lower vibrational level. This person may have had a great deal of suffering and your lack of respect will not help the situation, and most likely will makes things worst for this person. However, your respect will help this person as you are giving them a higher vibrational response, which may be all they need to turn things around and start heading up, instead of continuing to head lower.

One should always have consideration for others. Do not do to others anything that you would not want done to you. If you would not want someone to smash your car window, by all means do not do that to someone else. For several reasons, first it is wrong, it will pull you and the other person down vibrationally as this is a low vibrational type of action, and you will attract this same situation to yourself.

In regard to others, you should allow others to be that which they want to be, and you should not pay to much attention to them, just let them be. We must learn to accept others the way they are. If you do not like the way they are, just don't spend any time with them. It is not your duty to try and change someone else, they will seek help and change when they are ready. This is the problem with many relationships. A person meets someone else, they go out, start a relationship, and one person realizes the other person does not match their expectations, but they believe they can change the other person. This never works as you can not change someone else, they have to change themselves. The only person you really need to try and change is yourself.

Judgment

A judgment is an opinion or conclusion. So when you judge someone you are forming an opinion or making a conclusion about that person. As I mentioned earlier, you do not know what has happened to this person and why they are at a lower vibrational level. They may be going through a very difficult time in their life. By judging them you are not helping the situation. You are lowering their vibrational level and you are also lowering your own vibrational level. The best thing to do is have some understanding and show this person kindness, respect, and love. This may help the other person greatly. You do not have to become this persons best friend, you only have to be nice and kind to this person. Being kind to this person may be the exact thing this person needs to turn their life around. By being nice and kind you are making this world a better place for all.

Justification

If you say or do something to someone else, and you feel the need to justify what you said or did, then what you said or did is coming from a negative place. Justification is a way to cover up a negative statement or action. When you say or do something positive, there is never the need to justify your statements or actions. As a rule, always stay positive, positive speech and positive actions.

Forgiveness

Forgiveness is the act of forgiving someone for something they may have done to you or others. By not forgiving them you are creating negative energy and negative thought forms. This will cause negative emotions like anger, anxiety, bitterness, disappointment, fear, frustration, hatred, jealousy, resentment, stress, worry, and others. These things will only lower your own vibrational level. By not forgiving them you may be creating possible future unpleasant situations with this person. By forgiving them you are releasing this person and releasing any possible future situations. By forgiving them you are releasing all negative energy, thought forms, and emotions. You are also raising their vibrational level and raising your own vibrational level. Forgiveness is a high vibrational activity and state. Since we are trying to raise our own vibrational level, this is the best thing you can do for all people involved.

Life

Life is simple. Your life is made up of only two kinds of things, positive things and negative things.

Life is not suffering, it's just that you will suffer it, rather than enjoy it, until you let go of your mind's attachments and just go along for the ride. Your life is the way it is because of the choices you have made, or failed to make. When life's outcomes do not match our wishes, we feel threatened. Then our primary focus is on survival, so we are no longer focused on what we want, but on what we don't want or don't have. Then our motivation is based in fear and we move away from what we want rather than toward what we do want.

The way you are is not the result of what has happened to you, it is the result of what you decide to keep inside you. All permanent and lasting change must come from the inside. You are the creator of your own reality and life can show up no other way for you than that way in which you think it will. You think it into being. Change the old programs playing in your head to a new program and have a new lease on life. Handling negative attachments, if you really want to remove something from your life, you do not make a big production out of it, you just relax and remove it from your thinking. That's all there is to it. The thinking mind is a very powerful tool when used correctly, but when you let it take over your life, it is very limiting.

The mind is only a small aspect of the consciousness that you are. When you recognize that there is a voice in your head that pretends to be you and never stops speaking, you are awakening out of your unconscious identification with the stream of thinking. When you notice that voice, you realize that who you are is not the voice or the thinker, but the me who is aware of it. You are then knowing yourself as the awareness behind the voice, this is freedom.

Success, happiness, and good luck are available to any of us who are ready for it. Unfortunately, most of us do not know how to unlock the door. We sit and wait for our life to change, never realizing that the door to the prison is open. There are no guards. You may not be aware of it, but your attitude is either the key to open the door or the lock on the door. As I mentioned earlier, someone once said insanity is doing the same thing over and over, expecting a different result.

Remember, no matter how wonderful the present moment is, the future can be even more fulfilling and joyous. The universe always waits in smiling response for us to align our thinking with it laws. When we are in alignment, everything flows, anything is possible, you can do it, make the effort, you will be pleased. Your whole world will change for the better.

Two questions.

1. Have you found joy in your life.
2. Has your life brought joy to others.

The tragedy of life is not that it ends so soon, but that we wait so long to begin it. Here is a test to find out whether your mission on earth is finished. If you're alive, it isn't. Don't ask yourself what the world needs, ask what makes you come alive. Because what the world needs are people who have come alive. Have the courage to follow your dreams, that's your gift to the world. Don't spend your life wondering what could have been. Spend your time creating what could be.

Shakespeare said that life is our stage and we are all actors. The play must go on until you die. The only control you have over your life is changing the script. You can write a new script at any time. All it takes is a conscious decision to accept a new attitude. You can have your life be just the way you want it to be by choosing carefully the pictures you see in your mind's eye and the thoughts you put into your head. If you believe that you write the tale of your life, then the ending is also up to you. Destiny is not a matter of chance, it is a matter of choice. Life is only what you make of it. Do not seek to discover who you are, seek to determine who you want to be. Life is a process of creation, this is the greatest secret. Remember, there is no fate, but what we make for ourselves.

The past can only be remembered and the future has not happened. When the future does happen it is the now. So the everything that is real, is the now. The only thing that matters is what we are now and what we do now. When your attention moves into the now there is an alertness, it is as if you were waking up from a dream, the dream of thought, the dream of past and future. When your attention moves into the now there is just this moment as it is. As spiritual growth progresses, constructive life enhancing improvements in our personal circumstances naturally unfold because inner states of consciousness always reflect as outer conditions. Those of us who pay attention to the real reason that we're here begin to make an extraordinary impact on the world. Pay attention to the agenda of your soul, to the real reason that your here. There is only one purpose for your life and that is to experience yourself in your fullest glory. This life is just an experience, that's all it is.

Improving Life

Select one thing in your life that is not going well and which you wish to make successful, then treat it each day with selected thought. Spend up to fifteen minutes daily reconsidering the matter in the light of your knowledge of god. Remind yourself that harmony and true success are the divine purposes of your life. Realize that you are now knowing the truth about it and claim that the divine power in you is now healing the condition completely and permanently. Then give thanks for a complete demonstration. Give thanks and try to feel thankful. Mentally act the part of a person who has received this demonstration and is filled with gratitude. Repeat this until the demonstration comes. In between treatments you must keep your thoughts right concerning the subject. If it is possible, keep your thought off it altogether. You must not allow yourself to think wrongly concerning that subject. Remember that it is your mental agreement or acceptance that controls your life.

When the mind is strong and the heart is pure, your are free. It is the mind that connects you with pain in the body. When you think pure thoughts and are mentally strong, you can not suffer any painful effects. There are two ways to look at life. As though nothing were a miracle, or as though everything were a miracle. Fall in love with life. When you fall in love with your life, every limitation disappears. When you fall in love with life, you have no resistance, and whatever you love appears in your life almost instantaneously. You have to be alert to feel the love of everything around you. You have to be aware of everything that's around you. If you are walking down the street listening to the thoughts in your head, you miss it all. This is what is happening to people most of the time.

If you want to find the secrets of the universe, think in terms of energy, frequency, and vibration. You are either feeling good because you are full of love, or you are feeling bad because you are empty of love. All your feelings are degrees of love. All human action and reaction originates in either love or fear. Most people operate in or from fear. When you change the way you feel, you are on a different frequency, and the law of attraction responds instantaneously. You can harness the power of a good feeling to the fullest by turning up its volume. Deliberately intensify it so you feel as good as you can. The more you amplify your good feeling, the greater the love you give, the greater the results that you will receive back in your life, and these will be nothing short of spectacular. To amplify good feelings, think about things you love. Without exception, every person who has a great life used love to achieve it. The power to have all the positive and good things in life is love. When you choose to live in love, then you will experience the full glory of who you really are and who you can be. Every time you give love, you increase and multiply the love in the magnetic field around you. The more you give love and feel good, the more magnetic your field becomes and the more it expands, drawing everything and everyone you love to you.

Love is the greatest power in the universe. Love is not a feeling, love is a positive force. The more you feel love the stronger the magnetic field around you. You can get to a point where the magnetic power in your field is so positive and strong that you can have a flash of imagining and feeling something good, and within no time, it has appeared in your life, that is the power of love.

Living Your Greatest Life

Living a great life is not easy to do. In order to attract your biggest and greatest life, you must master applying the law of attraction. Do you want your life to truly take off, then change your ideas about it. Change your thoughts, words, and actions to match your grandest vision. If you want your life to take off, begin at once to imagine it the way you want it to be, and move into that. Check every thought, word, and action to ensure they are in harmony with the life you want. It is about finding inner peace and happiness, and attracting and manifesting your dream life. It is about living the life you were born to live. The ability to live life in harmony with your highest principles is one of the things which distinguishes humans from other animals. The true secret to life is to find love and peace within yourself and then share it with the world.

Never get tired of growing. When your mind is tired, exercise your body. When your body is tired, exercise your mind. Passion emerges from the heart and not from the mind. When you are confused, or lost, or don't know which direction to head, then just start walking and pay attention to what your heart tells you. If you live each day as if it were your last, someday you'll most certainly be right. Your time is limited. Don't let the noise of others opinions drown out your own inner voice and most important, have the courage to follow your heart and intuition. Everything else is secondary. Do what you love, follow your heart's direction and the path to fulfillment in life will naturally unfold before you.

The most difficult thing for people to do is to hear their own soul. Frustration comes from not listening to your own soul. Learn to follow the quiet voice within that speaks in feelings rather that words. Follow what you feel or hear inside. Let go of fear, worry, doubt, and disappointment. Listen to the voice within, this is god talking to you. You are divinely guided by spirit at all times. When there's a strong desire within you to express or create something, know that this is spirit telling you to take action and create. How many people get a chance to be their finest self. What do you have to be afraid of? If you were going to die in one year, what would you do? Make a list and do those things.

Breathing Exercise:

This breathing exercise is called "Relaxing breath". Please do this exercise everyday this week. The relaxing breath is a great relaxation technique. Inhale quietly through your nose and exhale loudly through your mouth. Begin the relaxing breath by exhaling through your mouth completely. Then inhale quietly through your nose for a count of eight, hold your breath for a count of six, and exhale loudly through your mouth for a count of four, let out a fast breath. Repeat for a total of five breath cycles. What is important here is the ratio of eight for inhalation, hold for six, and four for exhalation. After five breath cycles, breathe normally and notice how you feel. To get the long term benefits of the relaxing breath, do a minimum of five relaxing breathes twice a day. This is a very good technique if something upsets you, before you react, do this breath exercise to relieve the upset. It is also a very effective technique to cure anxiety.

Meditation Exercise:

For this meditation we will be using the spiritual eye often called the third eye. If you close your eyes, take a few deep breaths, and place your attention on the area between your two physical eyes, you will begin to see or feel an oval shaped object lying on its side, this is your spiritual eye or third eye.

This week we will continue using the Om mantra technique from the last chapter with one additional step. This week I would like you to also put your focus, attention, or concentration at the spiritual eye center or third eye between the eyebrows. The use of devotional prayer, breath awareness, listing to a mantra, and concentration at the spiritual eye center between the eyebrows are all helpful to quiet the mind.

Here is a review of this meditation. The manifestation symbol of god is Om. This is the Om Mantra technique. One should meditate on this word, contemplating and surrendering to it. Meditation on Om results in cosmic consciousness and the removal of all mental and physical obstacles to success on the spiritual path. With your eyes closed, look into the spiritual eye or third eye center, by concentrating at the spiritual eye center between your eyebrows. As you exhale, chant Om (O-o-o-o-o-m-m-n). Let it flow out easily, chant it quietly several times. Then after a while mentally chant Om going still more deeply within and listening in the inner ear canals to any subtle sounds that maybe discerned or heard. If you can actually hear a subtle continuous sound in your ears as though pervading your field of awareness, give your attention to that. Then cease mental chanting while continuing to listen to the mental sound resonating in your field of awareness, give attention to this sound. Please do this meditation twice a day for the entire week, in the morning when you first get up and again in the evening. For ten or fifteen minutes twice everyday, you should quiet the mind, close your eyes, and chant Om (O-o-o-o-o-m-m-n), while putting your focus, attention, or concentration at the spiritual eye center between the eyebrows.

Feelings and Emotions

Remove all feelings of not feeling good enough. For example if you feel you are not good enough to do some jobs well, then you will never get those jobs. Regain your confidence in yourself, feel good enough or better. Feel that you can do anything and by doing this you are sending out vibrations that will help you get what you desire. Enforced self discipline is controlling your emotions, taking control of your mind, positive mental attitude, and controlled enthusiasm.

Feelings and Emotions Exercise:

In this exercise you will spend ten or fifteen minutes everyday deliberately setting forth powerful thoughts that evoke great, powerful, passionate, positive emotion in order to attract what you want. Just sit still and quiet your mind, then concentrate on and fill your mind with powerful thoughts that evoke great, powerful, passionate, positive emotion in order to attract what you want. Pick something that you would like to bring into your life and work on that everyday during this week. This is also an exercise that you can use in the future whenever you wish to attract something into your life.

Habits

It takes twenty one days to create a new habit. Don't try and do everything at once. Choose one new habit, master it, then move on to another. If you keep doing what you have been doing, you will keep getting what you have been getting. If we get caught up in the small, day to day busy stuff, we could miss our chance to give the commitment needed to achieve the greater things in life. People who fail to achieve their real desires in life do so because they major in minor things. Sadly, most people never truly break their habits, no matter how hard they try. Year after year, they slip into the same patterns of thoughts, feelings, and behaviors. Failing by not doing, letting things happen in our lives, instead of directing our lives and determining our outcome. It is better to have tried and failed, then to have failed to try. When we live too much through our unconscious patterns, we create unconscious lives. The best way to predict our future is to create it. The end result is that we always attract what we feel worthy of. The truth of the matter is, in life you don't get what you want, you get what you expect.

Habits Exercise:

To create a good habit use the following exercise. To create a good habit, meditate for several minutes with concentration fixed at the christ center, also called the spiritual eye center or third eye, the point between the eyebrows, deeply affirm the good habit you want to install. The more you do this the more likely the good habit will stick. Pick one good habit you would like to install and use this exercise everyday for the next twenty one days, and then use this exercise as needed in the future.

Mind Exercise:

The seven day positive thought diet. This mind exercise called the seven day positive thought diet, is one that you will do for an entire seven days. We did a one day positive thought diet earlier in this book, but now we are going to do it for a full seven days. With just seven days of mild effort, you can change your life. So, for seven full days, change all your thoughts to positive creative thoughts. If a negative thought enters your mind, quickly notice it, and then quickly change it to a positive thought. If you see someone that stirs up negative thoughts, quickly notice it, and then quickly change it to a positive thought. If something happens that stirs up negative thoughts, quickly notice it, and then quickly change it to a positive thought. The goal here is to stop thinking negative thoughts and replace any negative thoughts with positive thoughts. All bad things that happen to us are attracted to us by our own negative thoughts. This one exercise by itself can have a profound impact on a persons life. Take this one day at a time. This exercise may take some effort. You may have to work yourself up to seven days. With seven days of mild effort, you can change your life. If you keep doing this for the entire seven days, it will become a very good habit that will change your life. The goal here would be to have only positive thoughts each and everyday for the rest of your life.

Mindfulness

When the energy of mindfulness is strong and you have concentration, you can practice looking deeply into the nature of whatever is arising, and from that comes insight. Insight liberates you from all negative tendencies. Breathing in, I know that I am breathing in, breathing out, I know that I am breathing out. You cultivate concentration, and with that concentration, you touch life deeply. You are at that moment free.

Mindfulness Exercise:

An entire day of mindfulness. Set aside one day every week or two to practice mindfulness. I said every week or two as once a week may be difficult to do, but try to do it at least once every two weeks. It may be best to do this on a day when you are not working and can put your full devotion to this mindfulness exercise. Do only simple work like house cleaning, garden work, cooking, washing clothes, washing your car, etc. and then take a slow motion bath. It is also good to meditate during the day. Every movement during this time should be at normal speed, not two times slower than usual. The point is to do one thing at a time at normal speed, keeping all of your attention on the one thing that you are doing and nothing else. Then move on to the next activity. Once again, every movement during this time should be at normal speed, keeping all of your attention on the one thing that you are doing and nothing else. Do this for a full day once every week or two. At end of the day sit in meditation for several minutes before going to bed. This exercise will help you pull your attention out of the past and the future, keeping you in the present. This exercise will take some effort. You may have to work yourself up to a day of mindfulness. See if you can do this a several times over the next few weeks. Once again, think of this as taking a vacation from yourself. You might like the change well enough to make it permanent. If an entire day is hard to do, you can start with half a day and work up to an entire day.

White Light

White light can be used for helping others. When you have a perception of someone else having a problem or a potential problem, you can imagine the person filled with white light and surrounded by white light, and hold the perception that this person is doing well. Rather than hold the perception of the problem, you should see the other person in white light, being happy, and being healthy. By holding that perception, you contribute to the co creation of physical reality.

White Light Exercise:

This white light exercise is called "Project love and white light ahead of you". As you go through your day, project love and white light ahead of you so that everywhere you go and everyone you meet will be filled with and full of love and white light. Simply project and cast forward love and white light so it touches and fills everything ahead of you. Try this exercise now. You should use this exercise often as you go through your day.

Additional Helpful Information – When You Can't Sleep

When you find it difficult to fall asleep at night, there are several natural things you can do to help you fall asleep. The first is massage the third eye point, at the spiritual eye center between the eyebrows. This is helpful when you have been doing much mental work before bed time. The second thing you can do is eat a snack, I find if I go to bed hungry, I have trouble falling asleep. The food pulls all of your energy into your stomach to process the food, allowing you to sleep. Next you can rub and massage your feet. There are points in your feet that when massaged will relax your body helping with the sleep process. You can also try taking a hot bath, as this will also help to relax your body, allowing you to sleep. If none of these work for you, try reading a good fantasy book, some fantasy fiction book about people and places of our imagination. Fantasy, or the unreal puts your mind into a relaxed and sleep like state. Next time you have trouble sleeping, try one or all of the above. You may need to find the one or two that work best for you.

Doing Nothing and Solitude

We live in a world where we are always doing something. We are constantly filled with thoughts and activities. One should take some time to just sit and be, to be still and reflect. Doing nothing will help pull you out of the rush of the material world so you can get in touch with your inner world, your spiritual side.

One should also seek solitude from the mental noise and vibrations of others. Sometimes when around too many people there can be so much mental chatter or noise that make it difficult to have a clear mind. This is why people feel better when they go to the country or out in nature, because this removes them from the mental noise and vibrations of others. When we are around too many other people, we tend to pick up on other peoples worries, fears, and doubt. We often confuse these feelings and thoughts of worry, fear, and doubt as our own. Seeking solitude on occasion will pull you out of or away from the mental noise, the feelings, and the vibrations of others. Remember, if we are around too many people of a lower vibrational level, we tend to have our vibrational level lowered. Solitude will help you clear your mind and allow you to hear your inner voice, thus raising your vibrational level.

Mass Consciousness

The planet is in the state it is in due to the mass consciousness of the planet, meaning the average consciousness or vibrational level of all the men and women on this planet. Unfortunately, the mass consciousness is still on the lower side, meaning there are still a great many people on the lower vibrational level. This is obvious when you look at what is happening in the world, we still have wars, we still have murder, we still have crime and corruption, and other activities of this nature. These are all lower vibrational activities. A high vibrational person would never take part in these types of activities.

Every person on the planet who raises their vibrational level helps the planet and helps man. This raises the average consciousness and vibrational level of all people, which raises the mass consciousness. As mass consciousness raises, there will be less war, less murder, less crime and corruption, and less of all the lower vibrational activities. By raising our vibrational level we pull all other people up with us and we raise the vibrational level of all other people. As we raise the vibrational level of the people around us, we raise the vibrational level of the entire planet. That would make this a much better planet to live on.

Remember, it is not your duty to try and change someone else unless they want your help. However, by raising your vibrational level you are indirectly helping others, you are helping to raise their vibrational level, even if they are not aware of it. Thus, it is the duty of every person who is spiritually aware to raise their vibrational level and help raise the mass consciousness of the planet and turn this into a better planet for all of us to live on. If one person gains spiritually, the whole world gains.

CONCLUSION

The vast majority of people sleep through their waking lives unaware of the powers within them. Capable of attaining spiritual heights, they seem to prefer the great dream of life instead of awakening to the true reality of themselves as a spark of the divine. We are lost in a dream, some would call us the sleeping man. One has to exercise the force of will in order to wake one self up in this lifetime. Other wise one drifts through life more or less in a sleep state missing most of the good stuff. Most of us allow the body, the emotions, and the mind to control our behavior and run our lives. We are spiritual beings. Most of us think we are human beings having a spiritual experience. However, it's actually the other way, we are spiritual beings having human experiences, not human beings having spiritual experiences. Because we are not the body, the emotions, or the mind, we must learn to take back control of these parts of us and not let them control us. We must be in charge of and in control of the body, the emotions, and the mind. We have for too long given control to the body, the emotions, and the mind, thus allowing these parts of us to run and determine the outcome of our life. When not in control, the body, the emotions, and the mind hinder our connection to our spirit, thus giving us lives that we really do not want because the outcome of our lives is not in our control. This is what is happening to most of us. By taking control back we can determine the circumstances and outcome in our lives and regain that connection with our spirit.

In this book we have learned how to be in control of our body, our emotions, and our mind. We have learned how to control our thoughts and be in charge of the thought process. We have learned how to control the creation process and create whatever we want in our lives. We have learned about living in the present moment, also called the now. We have learned about mindfulness and how to practice this in our lives. We have learned about energy and vibrations, and how these impact our relationships and our lives. We have also learned to be in control of all aspects of our lives and how to create the life that we want. Remember, we are spiritual beings having human experiences, not human beings having spiritual experiences.

If you have read the entire book, but have not done the exercises, I would suggest you go back and do all of the exercises. The only thing you have to lose is some of your time. However, by doing the exercises you will be receiving something far more valuable. You will learn how to reconnect with your true self, your spirit. Once the book is completed you should continue to do the exercises mentioned in this book, as they will lead to greater spiritual understanding and spiritual growth, and help you create a better life. The breathing exercises, the meditations, the work with emotions, exercises for the mind, work with thoughts, the use of mindfulness, and work with energy and vibrations are all activities you should do for the rest of your life. These are not activities that you do for two or three months and then stop, these are activities you do for a lifetime.

To create a better world, we must start with ourselves. Though no one can go back and make a brand new start, anyone can start from now and make a brand new ending. We are on planet earth because we have lessons to learn, have promises or agreements to keep, or a service to perform, or need to further awaken to our relationship with the infinite. We are where we are in time and space, and our circumstances are what they are because of our habitual states of consciousness, mental states, choices, and personal behaviors. Considering the matter of fate, the law of cause and effect or karma, we should acknowledge that what we have experienced, thought, and done in the past has produced our present circumstances. As travelers in the cosmic ocean of life, we are fated to wander in time and space, and to experience a variety of impermanent relationships and circumstances until, having discovered the truth about ourselves, we awaken from the dream of mortality and fulfill our spiritual destiny. Experiences of repeated physical birth and death continue until we out grow our attachments to this realm by awakening to higher realities.

Remember, there are six things you can do to help you regain the connection to your spirit, regain control of your life, and take back control of your life. These six things are:

1. Go within daily
2. Exercise the body
3. Eat well
4. Seek spiritual inspiration for your soul
5. Get sufficient sleep
6. Avoid drugs and alcohol

Man is a soul and has a body, several bodies in fact, for besides the visible vehicle by means of which he transacts his business with his lower world, he has others which are not visible to ordinary sight, by means of which he deals with the higher worlds. The layers of our selves are called maya koshas. Literally, maya means illusion and a kosha is a body sheath, a covering. So the ancients conceptualized the self as not one body but five distinct bodies layered on top of one another that cover the pure light of the highest self or the light within. Each body is a distinct maya kosha, or kosha for short. Each kosha is made up of increasingly finer energy vibrations as you move inward. These sheaths are often compared to layers of an onion that, over time, become so thick and hardened that they completely cover what's within. They become the obstacles that hinder our way to experiencing the sacred light. Some of us have trouble conceptualizing this inner light. Some people think of this deepest part of us as the soul, others call it god within, or their highest self. The first body is your physical body which we are all familiar with, this is the outer most body, the one you see. Your second body is your energy (breathing) body. Becoming aware of your flow of breathing is the first step in contacting your energy (breathing) body and an avenue into awareness of the deeper koshas. The third body is the mental (emotional) body, of the mind, senses, and emotions. Thoughts, feelings, and all that you perceive from the five senses reside within this kosha. Breathing techniques help keep this body in balance. Your fourth body, subtler still, is called your wisdom body. Your fifth body is called your bliss body. This is the subtlest body, the thinnest veil, which stands between ordinary awareness and the state of stillness, peace, bliss, and the light existing within us all. It helps to visualize them as sheaths, one on top of the other, with the first sheath, the physical body, on the outside, and the other layered successively within.

There's no single more powerful or more simple daily practice to further your health and well being than breath work. Breath is the great purifier, filling the blood with oxygen which each cell requires for internal breathing and repair. Correct breath is very important to our physical well being, our emotional state, our mental state, and our spiritual state. Its the breath that quiets the mind for meditation. Breath is the key. If we control the breath, we control the mind and the body. The breath is the master of the mind and body. Breath is the connection between mind and body. Breath work helps rise awareness, and helps turn your direction away from the material world to the non physical world.

Meditation means to think or look inwardly toward the soul, rather that outwardly through the senses. Meditation is a form of private devotion in which the mind concentrates on a particular practice which frees it from its normal thoughts. Meditation is the main vehicle for deepening one's spiritual life. Meditation is your way of staying connected to source, to god. By meditating, attention is removed from involvement with physical and mental processes. Through meditation, you free your body from slavery and acquire mastery over it. Meditation is communing with god for the purpose of working knowingly with god.

The phenomenon we call mind is the primary source of tension in our body, our emotions, and our daily lives. The mind forms a veil, an obscured lens, through which we see reality. We tend to accept these distorted perceptions as true and real until we realize that the mind itself is the mischief maker, the trickster, and the magician who weaves illusions while hiding in our psyche, whispering as friend and trusted adviser. The mind is the creator of illusion. The mind, or the mental body is the result of past thinking, and is constantly being modified by present thinking. In the building and evolution of our minds we must steadily work at right thinking, for we are our own builders. Thus the need for controlling our mind. Thought alone builds the mind. If your mind is filled with negative attitudes, it will be difficult to entertain positive attitudes. But if your mind is filled with positive attitudes, it will be difficult for negative ones to enter. We can not master our lives unless we master our minds. The soul seeks freedom from the prison of negative thinking.

Most people are not in charge of their own thoughts, and constantly bombard their higher self with an uncontrolled and contradictory mixture of plans, wishes, and fears. This confuses the higher self and is why most people's lives appear to be equally haphazard and uncontrolled, thus they don't get what they want. Most people spend there entire life imprisoned within the confines of their own thoughts. They never go beyond a narrow self created mind made sense of self that is conditioned by the past. Most people are not aware that we can control our state of mind by our thoughts. All things that manifest are preceded by the manifestation of thought, nothing just happens. Everything that happens is a vibrational response to a pattern of thought. Spiritually awakening is awakening from the dream of thought. You were born to live a good life, and you should start focusing your thoughts on things that will allow you to live a good life. That which you give your thought to is that which you begin to invite into your experience. You get what you are thinking about, whether it is something you want or something you do not want.

There is a network of energy that flows through all living things. Everything around us has energy. This energy forms the basis of and radiates outward from all things, including ourselves. We are subject to the energy that we are consciously or unconsciously radiating. The soul is life itself locally manifested, the soul is an individuation of the divine spirit which is all there is. The soul is universal life energy. The energy of universal life is often called the spirit or soul. We are energy units, we are energy. Human beings operate within a magnetic field. The human brain is both a broadcasting and a receiving station for vibrations of thought frequency. Learn to control your thoughts, for thought is energy. Man should strive gradually to redirect his energies upward from matter to spirit. The principle of vibration or resonance is the foundational basis of the universe, recognizing that all is energy or light. Universal laws function all the time on the principle of vibration and alignment. You are broadcasting and receiving vibrations to and from the world around you on a constant basis. The vibrations are formed by your thoughts, emotions, and life experiences. The goal is to get you to a place in your life where you are constantly in a positive state of mind, therefore constantly projecting positive energy. This positive energy will attract positive situations, people, and experiences into your life. We have a choice in life of either expanding or contracting our power. Anything positive, creative, or filled with love is expanding your energy, anything negative, destructive, or filled with hate and anger is contracting your energy.

The three levels or planes of existence are physical, mental, and spiritual. Each plane vibrates at different rates, and these vibrational differences are the only distinguishing factors between planes. The higher spiritual planes vibrate the fastest, and the lower material planes vibrate the slowest, which is why matter appears dense and solid. Each plane is divided into subcategories and is subdivided from lower to higher vibrations. The universe is in constant motion at different vibrations. The only variable separating one plane from another is its vibration. The higher the vibrational rate, the higher the plane. You are a vibration being. Every thought that you give your attention to expands and becomes part of your vibrational mix. Your attention to it invites it into your experience. This is an attraction based universe. If you want to find the secrets of the universe, think in terms of energy, frequency, and vibration.

The law of attraction states that thought energy and projected energy attract similar energy. As a result we attract things into our lives accordingly. We attract into our lives whatever we direct our conscious attention to. Like attracts like. The law of attraction asserts that, on a vibrational level, like attracts like. You are a living magnet, you attract into your life, the people, situations and circumstances that are in harmony with your dominant thoughts. You attract into your life whatever you give your attention and energy to, whether positive or negative. The law of attraction only responds to the vibration you are sending out right now. See yourself as a magnet, attracting unto you the way you feel. If you feel clear and in control you will attract clarity, if you feel happy you will attract happiness, if you feel healthy you will attract health, if you feel prosperous you will attract prosperity, if you feel love you will attract love.

Life is made of two realms, there is the inner world, and there is the outer world. Most of us only operate in the outer world, and don't even realize there is an inner world. We need to be connected to our inner world. Nothing is more fascinating than the journey of discovery into the world within. Everything that exists in the outer world begins in our inner most awareness.

Everything that is real, is the now. Give your attention to the moment, live in the now. It's always now. Surrender to the now, stop thinking, or at least stop paying attention to your thoughts. We are to live in the joyous moment, having given up attitudes and feelings of lack of worth, guilt over past actions (real or imagined), regret, fear, and anxiety. When your attention moves into the now there is an alertness, it is as if you were waking up from a dream, the dream of thought, the dream of past and future. When your attention moves into the now there is just this moment as it is. Focus your full attention on the here and now, not on the past or future. When you give your full attention to whoever or whatever you are interacting with, you take the past and future out of the equation. When you are doing something, your thoughts should be focused on what you are doing and nothing else. When you are doing nothing, your thoughts should be empty. Being in the here and now, the present, is the door to the kingdom of god. This will help transform your life and everything in it.

An emotion is energy in motion. Nothing rests, everything moves, everything vibrates. Your state of being is the way you feel about yourself at any point in time. Self esteem is merely feeling good about yourself, and when you do so, you develop confidence. Self esteem is what you think about yourself. Perfection in a human being means freedom from pain, suffering, doubt, and fear. Positive and negative emotions can not occupy the mind at the same time. One or the other must dominate. It is your responsibility to make sure that positive emotions constitute the dominating influence of your mind.

Mindfulness means observing, focusing your full attention on the here and now, not on the past or future. Focus a minute at a time, a thing at a time, on whatever catches our interest. This is what the Buddhists call living mindfully. Basically it means doing one thing at a time with your full attention on the one thing that you are doing. Do everything in a mindful state, meaning always put your attention and thought on what you are doing. Always be mindful, don't stay in your head. Keep your attention focused on what you are doing at that moment. Being in the here and now, the present, is the door to the kingdom of god. This will help transform your life and everything in it. Mindfulness is keeping one's consciousness alive to the present reality.

Our divine origin is spiritual love. Love is the source of all our power, of everything we need and desire. Love is the energy which expands, opens up, moves out, shares, and heals. You are either feeling good because you are full of love, or you are feeling bad because you are empty of love. All your feelings are degrees of love. All human action and reaction originates in either love or fear. Most people operate in or from fear. When you change the way you feel, you are on a different frequency, and the law of attraction responds instantaneously. When you choose to live in love, then you will experience the full glory of who you really are and who you can be. Love is the greatest power in the universe. Love is also the highest frequency or vibration. The feeling of love is the highest frequency or vibration you can emit. If you could wrap every thought in love, if you could love everything and everyone, your life would be transformed. Love is the power of the world. Every time you give love, you increase and multiply the love in the magnetic field around you. The more you give love and feel good, the more magnetic your field becomes and the more it expands, drawing everything and everyone you love to you. Without exception, every person who has a great life used love to achieve it. The power to have all the positive and good things in life is love.

We have the ability to create physical reality out of thin air. In the physical world you can not have a physical experience until you have created it first in thought. Negative emotion exists only when you are miss creating. When this happens stop doing whatever you are doing and focus your thoughts on something that feels better, something positive. The first level of creation is your thoughts. What you think produces energy in the universe, and if you think it often enough and long enough, it will actually produce a physical result in your life. The second level of creation is words. As you speak, so will it be done. Your word is really a form of energy. If you say something often enough, loudly enough, it will come to pass. Our actions are the third level of creation, that which we do. Life begins to change for you when you begin to say what you're thinking and do what you're saying. And then you have it all together and you start to create from all three centers of creation. Suddenly you begin to manifest and produce extraordinary results in your life in a very short period of time.

One of the greatest gifts you can give someone is your help. So I sincerely hope you will find this book a great help in reconnecting with your spiritual side. It is also my wish that this book help a great many people. With infinite love and light. Thank you.

INDEX

Printed in the United States
by Baker & Taylor Publisher Services